Twentieth-Century Jewelry

To Wagner and Etrusca

TWENTIETH-CENTURY JEWELRY

Art Nouveau to Modern Design

edited by
Lodovica Rizzoli Eleuteri

introductory essay by
Annamaria Massinelli

photographs by
Alessandro Parenti

Electa/Abbeville
Milan   New York

Translation
Huw Evans

Graphic Design
Marcello Francone

Impagination
Dario Tagliabue

Front Cover
Bracelet-watch in yellow gold with a small sky-blue hemisphere at the center decorated with diamond-studded stars (Rolex watch), *circa* 1940. Private Collection.

ISBN 1-55859-775-1

© 1994 by **Electa**, Milan
Elemond Editori Associati

All rights reserved under international copyright conventions. No part of this book may be reproduced or utilized in any form or by any means, electronic or mechanical, including photocopying, recording, or by any information storage and retrieval system, without permission in writing from the publisher. Inquiries should be addressed to Abbeville Publishing Group, 488 Madison Avenue New York, N.Y. 10022.
Printed and bound in Italy.

First U.S. edition

The editor of this volume would like to express her gratitude to all those who have contributed to the realization of the work.
Particular thanks go to Christie's and Sotheby's, the Maisons Boucheron, Gian Maria Buccellati, Bulgari, Cartier, Carlo Eleuteri, Mauboussin, Mellerio dit Meller, Erminio Rizzoli (Herriz), Seaman Schepps, Van Cleef & Arpels, Claudio Zanettin, and Carlo Ferrero Zendrini, for having placed their photographic archives at our disposal and for having allowed us to photograph some of the jewelry in their collections.
She would also like to thank all the private collectors who have kindly given permission for us to photograph their jewelry. Thanks are also due to those who have contributed to the success of this volume: Emanuela and Tiziana Appetiti, Susanna Benvenuti, François Canavy, Gabriella Longo, Ennio Parrelli, Virgilio Pulsoni, Pauline Schaefer, Natalie Vianello Chiodo, and in particular Sante Polica.

Contents

7 From Art Nouveau to Artist's Jewelry
Annamaria Massinelli

30 Extraordinary Jewels:
An Adventure Beyond Style
Lodovica Rizzoli Eleuteri

Catalogue

37 The First Twenty Years
of the Century

51 The Twenties and Thirties

89 From the Forties to the Sixties

149 Index of Jewelers

Publisher's Note
Annamaria Massinelli contributed to the
chronological arrangement of the section
on "Extraordinary Jewels" and to the revision
of its captions.
Lodovica Rizzoli Eleuteri tracked down and selected
the material in the same section, and wrote the
captions.

From Art Nouveau to Artist's Jewelry

Annamaria Massinelli

The Decline of Jewelry in the Antique Style

In 1841 Georg Carl Backes (1819-1890), a goldsmith from Hanau, prepared to set out on what was perhaps one of the most important experiences in his life: a journey that, with stops along the way, had as its final goal the city of Florence.[1] In those years a visit to that city was obligatory at some time in the life and career of an artist: in fact, the masterpieces of old, the great works of the Renaissance, were regarded as a source of new inspiration for their creativity.

Much later, in 1874, Backes brought back from that experience a precious store of meticulously drawn sketches tinted in watercolor (Hanau Zeichenakademie), made from one of the most prestigious collections in Europe: that of the precious objects from the Medicean treasury, assembled at the time in the Sala delle Gemme in the Uffizi (and now in the Museo degli Argenti). Old pieces of jewelry and cameos, with elaborate settings of enameled gold, together with vases made of semiprecious stones with handles cast in the shape of harpies, dragons, and dolphins, all figure in Backes's drawings, on which the goldsmith scrupulously noted down an attribution that is debatable today: Benvenuto Cellini. The craftsman got more ideas from Vienna, where he was able to admire other masterpieces of Renaissance goldwork, such as the detail of the hilt of Emperor Charles V's sword.

This eager attempt at "renovation" tells us a great deal about the cultural baggage and stylistic orientation that had guided the work of the generation of goldsmiths to which Backes belonged. The panorama of jewelry in the traditional style in the historicist climate of the *demi-siècle* included examples of unquestionably high craftsmanship: the stimulus of the past had given rise to the invention of some surprising objects. One thinks of the neo-medieval collar with rubies, diamonds, turquoises, pearls, and a Gothic inscription, designed by the English architect A.W. Pugin (London, Victoria and Albert Museum), or the experiments in an archeological manner by the Roman goldsmith Pio Fortunato Castellani (1793-1865), his brother Augusto (1829-1914), and son Alessandro (1823-1895), as well as by another famous imitator of the antique, Carlo Giuliano (1831-1895). These last, under the influence of the discoveries of ancient Etruscan, Roman, Greek, and Byzantine goldwork, tried to understand the secrets of their predecessors' craft. Thus Pio Fortunato Castellani spent years, together with the archeologist Michelangelo Caetani, studying the casting techniques of the Etruscans. He was especially interested in discovering the secret of the soldering that permitted the creation of extremely fine objects decorated with a granular effect, such as the ones found in the Etruscan tombs of Caere and collected by the archeologist Cavalier Campana, who possessed almost a thousand precious ornaments of archeological origin.[2]

In France François-Désiré Froment-Maurice looked back to the Gothic and Renaissance masterpieces of his own land, and showed a particular preference for lively ornamentation: his brooches and bracelets are decorated with little scenes based on stories from the romances of chivalry, along with putti and allegorical figures, all squeezed into the limited space of a piece of jewelry and yet attaining the dignity of a work of sculpture.

Jewelry in an Italian archeological style went through a period of brief but intense popularity in France as well.

Alessandro Castellani was in Paris in June 1860. He opened a school of archeology for jewelers on the Champs-Elysées, which was supposed to revive "the ornaments of the heroes and the divinities of whom Homer sang, those of the beauties of Mycenae, Cyprus, and Tyre." This was the line taken by the jewelers on show at the London Exhibition of 1862, a prestigious occasion at which Castellani would be given the credit for the revival of Greek, Etruscan, and Roman jewelry. A lecture that he gave in Paris was also translated into English and published at this time, under the title *Antique Jewelry and its Revival*. For other exhibitors as well, including Marret et Baugrand, Phillips of London, Mellerio, and Casillot, the novelty lay in antique jewelry.[3]

The Parisian goldsmith Eugène Fontenay (1824-1887) was one of those most greatly impressed by Castellani's creations and by the antique collection of Marchese Campana. This was exhibited at the Louvre in 1861, prompting the painter Jean-Auguste-Dominique Ingres to write: "There are some things of a totally new kind that come as a surprise to those who believe they are familiar with antiquity."

Yet not much time passed before Fontenay himself, in his treatise *Les bijoux anciens et modernes* published in Paris in 1887, was forced to admit that the fickle taste and frenetic life of a society accustomed to the rapid pace of industrialization could not wait for the results of the slow process of experimentation carried out by cultivated craftsmen like the Castellani: "Nervous and impatient, with no time to look at anything, it behaves as if every day that passes had no tomorrow."

It is clear, moreover, that the Etruscan-style lockets and necklaces proposed by Fontenay, or his amphora-shaped earrings, conveyed aesthetic messages, ethical models, and cultural allusions that meant little to the bourgeois woman of the end of the century, who was completely intoxicated by the lively fashionable society of Paris, liberated from her crinoline, and fascinated by the new developments that were emerging, from one side of Europe to the other, in the codes of ornamentation. The modern woman was much more strongly attracted by the new cultural trademarks, art nouveau and Jugendstil.

The exhibitions of the closing decades of the century provided confirmation of the growing international character of jewelry, with the products of European firms competing directly with those of American producers. At the Universal Exhibition of 1899, Tiffany presented a range of enameled brooches studded with precious stones. So naturalistic was their effect, in the shades of color as well as the movement of the petals, that they looked like freshly picked flowers. However the production of this workshop was characterized by the use of large colored stones or diamonds, which had become available in large numbers on the market since the opening of the African mines in 1870. From this point of view, they were perfectly in harmony with the products of Cartier. "Essentially we use stones and very few other materials,"[4] declared Pierre Cartier, underlining the aristocratic style that was still a mark of expensive jewelry, in contrast to the other, non-precious materials that art nouveau was bringing onto the market and to the themes of the new *décor* that were attracting the interest of a broad clientele of varied social extraction. Since 1870 in fact, the *genre anglais*, developed in connection with the passion for horse racing and characterized by jewelry made of yellow gold in the shape of horseshoes, horse's heads, or stirrups, had become very common. Alongside these forms based on animals there was another current that took its inspiration from fantastic subjects or from a naturalism with shadowy tones (Cartier's inseparable little parrots on a branch). Flowers also figured in the repertory of the major Parisian jewelers even before the last decade of the century. However the art nouveau style was to completely alter

François Kramer, Brooch for Empress Eugenie, in platinum and diamonds, 1855. Private Collection.

Parure consisting of necklace and rose-cut diamonds, second half of nineteenth century. Herriz Collection.

Brooch in the form of an eagle perched on a branch, in yellow gold and diamonds, partially enameled and decorated with diamonds, rubies, emeralds, 1880s. Herriz Collection.

their significance: plants, birds, and insects were proposed from a very different viewpoint, with a graphic definition of outlines and veining, in an effort of stylization that almost clashed with the refined picturesque effect obtained through the use of materials such as enamel and glass, bone, ivory, and synthetic resins, or semiprecious stones like opal, long neglected by high-class jewelry. Twenty years after Charles Blanc had dismissed the reproduction of parts of the human body as being of poor taste in his *L'art et la parure dans le vêtement* (1875), the range of favorite art nouveau subjects included an ideal feminine image proposed in a wide variety of forms, but that reflected the aspirations of ordinary women through an aesthetic canon that conveyed a message of renewal. A woman with regular, harmonious, and resolute features, unconstrained in the movement of her body, swathed in light and fluttering fabrics, and with hair that was loose and flowing, rather than imprisoned in a rigid *coiffure*. Woman as mistress of nature, blended with plants and insects in an allusion to a concrete metamorphosis of life that, within the space of few decades, was to see her victorious. Line and color, rather than volume: woman and the natural world became the mark of many Parisian trends as the century drew to a close.

Women, Insects, and Flowers or Garland Style?

Among the historical styles that had come back into vogue since the middle of the nineteenth century, the revival of Louis XV and Louis XVI *décors* was perhaps the most deeply rooted, so that even in the nineties the repertories of the most important ornamentalists of the eighteenth century were being reprinted in their entirety. The *maisons* of Cartier, Vever, or Mellerio dit Meller drew extensively on such models, as they had to meet the requirements of an aristocratic clientele, at the European courts or among the *nouveaux riches*, even on the other side of the Atlantic. Such customers were more willing to entrust the ostentation of their prestige to stately creations in the garland style that conjured up echoes of the court of Versailles.[5]

Diadems, necklaces, and bodice orna-

Alphonse Fouquet, "Bianca Capello" châtelaine, in gold, diamonds, and enamel, circa 1878. Paris, Musée des Arts Décoratifs.

ments with rigidly symmetrical designs were the most popular types. A recurrent motif for brooches was the bow with tassel-shaped pendants. Another style that had aroused Louis Cartier's enthusiasm was that of jewelry worked in the manner of lace and embroidery. The ideal metal was white: silver or, even better, platinum. Even the stones had to fit in with the purity of the metal, without strong contrasts, and so pearls and diamonds were preferred.

The courts of Europe continually provided occasions for the display of jewelry of consequence: birthdays, weddings, and prestigious celebrations of various kinds. Even in the years when the Wiener Werkstätte was advocating the use of materials like silver and semiprecious stones and a renewal of forms, the Koechert family of jewelers in Vienna, purveyors to the Austrian imperial house, stuck to its traditional and sumptuous production. A selection of eighty-two pieces, presented to the Viennese public between 1909 and 1911, won the approval of the critics, who appreciated the quality and value of the jewelry on show, although the total absence of modernistic elements was noted.[6]

The London jewelers, Garrard, that supplied the English royal house, the Milanese Annibale Cusi and Capello of Turin, suppliers of the House of Savoy, and Carl Fabergé who worked for the Romanovs, all adopted the conventions of the garland style.

Attempts at a renewal of this kind of jewelry had been made by Vever who, in a number of tiaras dating from 1900 (Paris, Musée des Arts Décoratifs), made use of an asymmetrical plaitwork of plants.[7] In an example from 1908, Georges Fouquet, although adopting a traditionally symmetrical design, made use of strong color contrasts with enamel decorations or large aquamarines combined with pearls (Paris, Musée des Arts Décoratifs). A large variety

Castellani, Parure with pearls, rubies, emeralds, and cameos from the end of the sixteenth century. Private Collection.

Maison Vever, "Silvia" pendant, in gold, agate, rubies, diamonds, and enamel, circa 1900. Paris, Musée des Arts Décoratifs.

of diadems were produced by the Maison Cartier: some had an intricate motif, such as a sunburst centered on a large stone, with an interlacing pattern of olive or laurel leaves, or of sprigs of wheat, while others had a series of plaitwork motifs that included, as pendants, stones cut into the shape of drops. The Kokosnik, or Russian diadem, had a compact form that Cartier had tried to lighten with perforations ornamented by stones. The most bizarre type was the winged diadem, consisting of two naturalistic wings with a large gem in the middle.[8] After the end of the First World War however, this production began to decline, even though sporadic commissions for tiaras did continue up until the thirties; only the English court has stuck tenaciously to this model of jewelry until recent times.

Toward the end of the century Rue de la Paix, with the adjacent Place Vendôme, became a magnet for the most elegant society. Fashionable couturiers, like Worth, and the leading jewelers moved their workshops here: Mellerio dit Meller, Vever, Aucoc, Boucheron, and Lalique; in 1899 Cartier too moved his premises from Boulevard des Italiens to Rue de la Paix.

The frequent visits of illustrious clients attracted crowds of curious onlookers, thronging the most chic sidewalks in Paris, anxious not to miss the spectacle of the arrival of the Aga Khan, Baroness de Rothschild, or King Edward VII. The store windows, crammed with sparkling and spectacular jewelry, displayed creations in line with the avantgarde taste of the last decade of the nineteenth century alongside the classic garland style.

Art nouveau jewelry, naturalistic and asymmetrical, peacefully coexisted with the courtly garland style which, it could be said, has never been completely eclipsed in high-class jewelry. However the more traditional techniques and materials did not permit the aesthetic requirements of the art nouveau style to find a satisfactory expression. Jewelers, like other artists, wanted to convey the sensuality and colors of nature and an impression of dynamism, even if it were the more superficial one of a society touched by the magic wand of industrialization. The counterpart to the whirling rhythms of a dancer like Loïe Fuller, the muse of many artists, to the brightly colored and magical atmosphere of the theaters that every evening offered stimulating performances of ballets, music, or shadow plays, was not to be found in the pompous sets in the garland style, at least according to the principal champions of art nouveau jewelry, René Lalique and Georges Fouquet.

The frequent exhibitions and the more avant-garde reviews contributed to the diffusion of models and ornaments for objects in the new style. In Paris, these could be purchased at the well-stocked store of Siegfried Bing, "Art Nouveau," or that of the German Julius Meier Graefe, "La maison moderne."

The jewelry on offer in these two galleries attracted the attention and curiosity of customers in part through its use of non-precious materials, such as horn carved and painted in soft colors, or covered with a coating of silver.

The criterion on which these jewels were judged was no longer simply that of the value of the materials used, but the originality and quality of the design and the refinement and difficulty of the techniques employed.

For this reason objects made out of enameled gold, even without precious stones, produced by Georges Fouquet or René Lalique (1860-1945), could fetch truly exorbitant prices.

René Lalique's initial training as a painter, who sought his inspiration in the observation and study of nature, and went on to create refined plaques of ivory decorated with flowers and insects, was fundamental to his later activity as a designer of jewelry. The debut of the young and former aspiring painter in the world of jewelry took place in 1876, the year in which he began his apprenticeship with Louis Aucoc, with whom he remained until 1878.

During the three years that he spent in London at the end of this period, the artist became involved in the debate stirred up by the Arts and Crafts movement, although his life at Sydenham College, devoted chiefly to study, kept him out of the principal cultural and society events in the capital.

Lalique, however, seems to have instinctively absorbed the atmosphere of those years: in any case the questions over which critics and theorists argued so passionately attracted his attention. The equality of the arts and the dignity of all the materials employed were concepts fundamental to the work of the artist who, after starting with painting, had then learned the techniques of goldsmith's work, studied sculpture under Justin Lequien, and learned how to work glass.

Thanks to this many-sided training and an indefatigable imagination, Lalique managed to design jewelry that, when exhibited at the National Exhibition of Industrial Arts held in Paris in 1887, appeared downright revolutionary and was therefore little understood and appreciated.

Fascinated by the iridescent colors of insects and the fleeting reflections of light, the artist had tried to convey the same sensual effects in his jewelry, using enamel, glass, and semiprecious stones like chalcedony and opal, the stone of which Cartier had such a poor opinion. The chromatic effects that he succeeded in creating were amazing and impressed the actress Sarah Bernhardt. The result was that he was swept along on the crest of her celebrity. The last decade of the nineteenth century brought him a series of successes and achievements, culminating in the award of the Légion d'Honneur at the 1897 Salon de Paris, while in the first decade of the following century the artist's fame spread throughout Europe. The celebrated bodice brooch he created for the "divine Sarah" is in the shape of a gecko, with a long tapering body and large claws. Out of its mouth emerges a female torso carved out of ivory, with large dragonfly wings instead of arms. The animal's body is decorated with chrysoprases, the wings with enamel, using the *pliqué-à-jour* technique, and diamonds (Lisbon, Gulbenkian Foundation). The method of applying enamel adopted by Lalique, and by other contemporary jewelers, made it possible to achieve extraordinary effects of transparence, since the honeycomb cells to which the glass paste was applied had no bottoms. Another jeweler who was extremely fond of enamel decorations, Lucien Falize (1839-1897), obtained very different effects in his enameled jewelry in a historicist style or even, in the eighties, with art nouveau motifs: in this case the glass paste was poured onto metal plates, where thin fillets or *cloisons* shaped it into enameled ornamental patterns of different colors.[9] The *pliqué-à-jour* technique was used by Lalique for petals and flowers as well, creating an incomparable effect of lightness. An example of this is the large lotus flower he designed for Bernhardt. In the years when Lalique was heading toward success and recognition of the undisputed artistic value of his work,[10] a range of costume jewelry of a more commercial character was being developed. These made use of the whole range of ornamental solutions adopted by art nouveau, employing a wide variety of techniques and inexpensive materials. The Parisian firm Piel Frères substituted copper and silver for gold, and celluloid for ivory, while in Great Britain and America a type of cheap jewelry taking its inspiration from the

René Lalique, "The Kiss" brooch in ivory, gold, and enamel. Lisbon, Museu Calouste Gulbenkian.

art nouveau style was now being produced on a large scale. Hat pins, buckles, and combs for fixing hairstyles, together with brooches, necklaces, and bracelets, seem to have been the most common kinds of ornament.[11]

Alongside the products of a cheaper kind that slavishly copied the art nouveau repertory of forms, original and valuable designs of jewelry continued to appear, some of them achieving, on the level of creativity, the quality of Lalique's works.

Georges (1862-1957), the son of Alphonse Fouquet (1828-1911), went along with the new trends in taste, abandoning the style of his father, who had specialized in neo-Renaissance jewelry. His reputation was also linked with the "divine" Sarah Bernhardt who, while playing the role of Cleopatra, wore a fanciful piece of jewelry made by Fouquet: the celebrated bracelet in the form of a coiled serpent, in enameled gold, opal, and rubies (plate 1). This bizarre invention had been designed by Alphonse Mucha who, as well as collaborating with the jeweler, designed posters for the actress.

Ever since the seventies, Frédéric Boucheron (1830-1903) had had great success in the United States with his jewelry strongly influenced by historicist styles. His fame would later be crowned by commercial success in Russia and Britain. In the last decade of the century he adapted to the now rampant art nouveau style, seeking to reconcile the new themes with a rigorous design and the use of traditional materials. In his insects and flowers he made constant use, along with enamel, of precious stones: diamonds, rubies, and sapphires. At times, while not renouncing the use of these gems, he succeeded in achieving remarkably naturalistic effects, as in the butterfly-shaped brooch with its body made out of a ruby and four diamonds on which the veins of the wings are engraved.[12]

Buckles and brooches were often made out of cast gold, with ornamental motifs such as women's heads or monstrous animals, panthers or dolphins, arranged in a symmetrical manner and with large gems set at their centers. At the beginning of the twentieth century the Maison went back to producing more traditional jewelry as well, once again offering bows in platinum, darkened steel, and diamonds, with a lace-like effect (plate 10), or necklaces in the Régence style.[13]

The production of the Maison Vever, where since 1821 Pierre, Ernest, Paul, and Henri had succeeded one another at the helm of the firm, also made a fairly conventional adaptation to the art nouveau style of decoration. The themes of the iris, carnation, mistletoe, peacocks, and female figures appeared on buckles, brooches, combs, and pendants, in a wide variety of combinations. The jewelry, often cast in yellow gold, was given a lively and delicate appearance by refined polychrome enamel decorations and the insertion of precious stones and opals. It was not rare for ivory to be used, as in a sunflower-shaped pendant overlaid with a female profile with disheveled hair.

We are also indebted to Henri Vever for an invaluable repertory of French jewelry of the nineteenth century in three volumes, published in Paris between 1906 and 1908. Even today this remains a fundamental work for students of jewelry and provides an accurate picture of Vever production. The panorama presented by this goldsmith in his treatise shows us how the great boulevards of Paris were lined with the glittering store windows of a myriad of jewelers in search of ever newer and more bizarre inventions: Louis Aucoc, where René Lalique had started his career as an apprentice, Falize Frères, Eugène Feuillâtre, Lucien Gaillard, Piel Frères, and Edouard Colonna were among the best-known names.

René Lalique, Necklace in horn and pearls, 1902-4. Lisbon, Museu Calouste Gulbenkian.

Tiffany, Bodice ornament in the form of an iris, with 139 sapphires, diamonds, and topazes, shown at the Universal Exhibition in Paris in 1900. Baltimore, Walters Art Gallery.

In the first decade of the twentieth century, magazines like *Art et décoration*, *L'art décoratif*, *The Studio*, or *Die Kunst* contributed to the diffusion of forms and ideas with their illustrations, aiming to keep alive and regenerate a type of ornamentation whose possibilities seemed infinite.

The attempt to establish a firm underpinning, even in scientific terms, to the new tendency in decoration found concrete form in plates showing sections and details of plants, such as mistletoe or orchids, while studies of the movement of the frog were used as starting points for the design of vases.

In 1904 *Art et décoration* made an appeal for a more thorough study of the ideas for ornamentation that could be derived from the observation various species of insects, and not just dragonflies and butterflies, "since for the decorator, the word insect usually means butterfly." Yet even flies could be a source of creative inspiration: in their eyes could be found the strange magic of an iridescent mosaic of stones. It was under the influence of this kind of scientific and naturalistic investigation that, in the year 1903, Boutet de Monvel published an illustration of a necklace ornamented with a row of peas in the pages of *L'art décoratif*.

In the Italian city of Trieste, Leopoldo and Giuseppe Janesich were producing refined jewelry in the art nouveau style. The goldsmith Vincenzo Miranda, who was active in Naples from 1889, moved away from antique jewelry, still in vogue in that city, and made an impression at the Turin exhibition of 1902 with more modern "liberty" creations, as the art nouveau style was called in Italy. The same trend can be seen in the designs of Giorgio Ceragioli (1861-1947). Also a decorator of fabrics, he produced jewelry for the Musy firm, and was one of the suppliers to the court aristocracy. The need to come up with more and more surprising inven-

tions grew even more pressing as a result of the frenzied rate of production in those years, which often made it difficult to avoid repetition. In 1906 the series of gaudy enameled eggs that Carl Fabergé had been designing and producing for the tsars in Russia aroused great admiration when they were put on show in Paris. It seems that no one had come up with such an original idea in the area of curios for many years. The model remained a specialty of the St. Petersburg firm, even though Cartier made two eggs for Tsar Nicholas II in 1906 and 1907. The Parisian Maison immediately sensed the possibility of finding some completely new ideas in Russian production and, after a trip by Pierre Cartier to St. Petersburg and Moscow in 1904 and 1905, links were established with various workshops—Yahr, Woerffel, Ovcinikov, and Denisov-Uralski—for the supply of objects made out of jade or other semiprecious stones or out of enameled gold, along with jewelry in animal forms. The Cartiers were in any case ready to look almost anywhere for ideas that might lead to the design of jewelry that would stand out for its elegance and originality, without necessarily drawing on the repertory of art nouveau. India, for example, turned out to be another fertile source of inspiration. At the Universal Exhibition of 1900 Cartier exhibited an "Indian" ring ornamented with two emeralds *en cabochon*. After 1910, under the influence of Jeanne Toussaint and in parallel with the trend in fashion set by the couturier Poiret, this style turned out to be one of the most popular. Emerald was the stone most suited to jewelry in the Indian style, along with carved *boules* made from a variety of stones: sapphires, rubies, tourmaline, onyx, and turquoise, and even amber and coral. Undoubtedly, however, the type of jewelry that most effectively conjured up the mysterious world of the maharajas was that of the *aigrette*, or spray of jewels used as a head ornament. These would sometimes bear, on a base of precious metal and gems, a tuft of rare and very light feathers.

In the multifaceted range of exotic influences that it was able to embrace, the output of Cartier, with the exception of sporadic examples supplied to the firm by other goldsmiths, slipped almost untouched between garland style and art deco. In any case, at the height of the effort to renew traditional ornamentation, even the aspirations of art nouveau fell by the wayside. Pointless labor and time wasted, for the objective of the new generation was that of the clean line, of sharp outlines. This was how Adolf Loos, in almost lapidary terms, set the seal on the end of one era and the beginning of another: "Ornamentation is wasted effort and there-

Tiffany, Necklace with pendant-brooch, in gold with enamel, sapphires, topazes, amethysts, and pearls, circa 1910. Tiffany Collection.

Maurice Dufrène, Drawings of art nouveau jewelry.

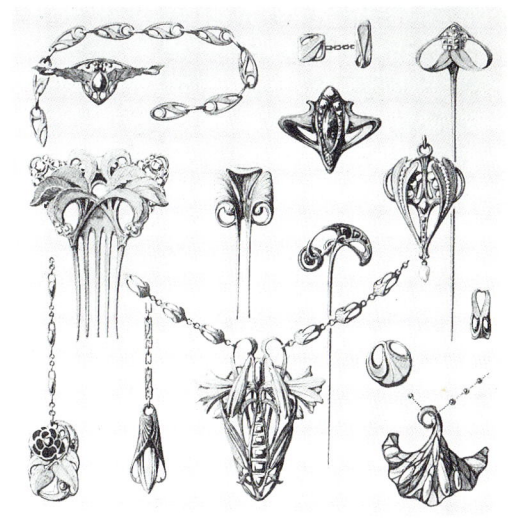

fore a waste of health. It has always been so. But today it means a waste of material as well, and the two things together mean a waste of capital."[14]
Although in a genre like that of jewelry, ornamentation in itself was little affected by Loos's last argument, it was intimately bound up with general trends in taste, and the effects were evident.

Geometric Fantasies
In the first decade of the new century, the Parisian couturier Paul Poiret had proposed some eccentric and revolutionary designs, which showed a marked tendency to verticality.
With curves banished, the clothing of the twenties, light and based on masculine styles, was suited to the slender and long-limbed woman, obliging the less fortunate to squeeze themselves into very tight girdles to reduce any impression of rotundity as much as possible.[15]
The fascination with the East played a far from minor part and the myth of the odalisque, her head covered with a turban and ornamented by an eccentric *aigrette* and wearing long, fancy tunics, was nurtured by Paul Poiret through the models he proposed in the fashion magazines of the day, while the Turkish pants he made for his wife in 1911, for a party on the theme of *A Thousand and One Nights*, caused a sensation.
Mysterious women, looking like they had just come out of a fairy tale, were the source of inspiration for the covers designed by Erté for *Harper's Bazaar* during the First World War, as well as in the twenties.[16] Sophisticated designs were used for evening wear: the emancipated *garçonne* appeared in unisex clothes and a very short haircut in the afternoon, but in the evening she relied for her seductive wiles on dresses in the Oriental style, on mischievous and uninhibited necklines and slits that, with nonchalance, allowed glimpses of an accessory that was sometimes as precious as a jewel: "A large Chinese bow

Koechert, Drawing of necklace for the actress Katharina Schratt, circa 1910.

hung in a drapery full of good taste, that left uncovered as far as the garter, secured with a diamond, a nimble leg with harmonious Tuscan curves."[17]

In the realm of head ornaments the diadem was gradually replaced by the *bandeau*, of which occasional examples were to be found even before the First World War. Conceived as a narrow band, slipped over the forehead, it was perfectly in tune with the masculine fringes and the geometric severity of the deco style. It could even be used as a bracelet or transformed into a brooch or clip. Suitable earrings had large pendants, possibly in the form of teardrops. The elegant woman of the twenties, liberated from the nineteenth-century bodice, matched her soft and willowy garments with long necklaces of pearls, while equally long ropes of pearls were wound several times around her wrist. The triumph of the pearl dated from the years before the war. The early years of the twentieth century saw a succession of fabulous sales, and prices for natural pearls, from the second decade onward, were on a par with those of the greatest masterpieces of painting. But perhaps all that is needed to convey an idea of just how prized they were is to tell the famous story of Pierre Cartier's purchase of the great six-story Renaissance-style building on Fifth Avenue, which then became his New York headquarters. He paid for it with two precious ropes of pearls desired by Mrs. Plant, the wife of the banker with whom he made the exchange. The deal is one of the most brilliant examples of the Parisian jeweler's farsightedness, for only shortly afterward, following the crash of 1929, the value of pearls fell steeply. In addition the growing availability of cultured pearls produced in Japan, although spurned by the major jewelers, had seriously depressed the market for natural ones.

The great vogue for long strings of pearls in the twenties was responsible for the popularity of alternative solutions, in the following decade as well: less expensive cultured pearls, invented by Kokichi Mikimoto, took their place alongside the imitation ones, in a wide variety of colors.

From 1922 onward, they began to be used not only for very long necklaces or *bandeaux* worn on the forehead, but also to decorate evening dresses. Paul Poiret's creations had showy side decorations with great cascades of pearls.

To adapt to this new and lanky image of woman, designers of jewelry borrowed styles from a variety of sources: the Wiener Werkstätte, the currents of Cubism and Futurism, the Bauhaus, and cultural events of international significance, such as the new archeological discoveries in Egypt (Tutankhamun's tomb was brought to light in 1922).

Even Filippo Tommaso Marinetti, in 1930, temporarily set aside his image as the founder of Futurism to write a nostalgic work, *Il fascino dell'Egitto*, conjuring up the sights, colors, sounds, and forms of one of the countries that had most caught the imagination of Europeans: "Master the uncovered geometry of the bowels of the desert all cubes spheres triangles cones of calcified bladders muscles. Tall sparks of green gold flicker on the merlons of the walls that appear to drip with a torrid blue milk."[18] Endless fantasies of color were also to be found in the choreographies of Sergei Diaghilev. His production of Rimsky-Korsakov's *Sheherazade* in Paris in 1910 had such a powerful influence on the taste of those years that it affected developments in many sectors of the decorative arts, but other influences came from African, Chinese, Japanese, and Persian art. Jewelers responded to this both in their combination of materials and by their adoption of all the possible forms that derived from the cultural trends of the moment. The soft and iridescent tones preferred by art nouveau gave way to sharper contrasts of color obtained through a combination of precious and semiprecious stones: black onyx and diamond was one of the favorite couplings of art deco. Agate, jade, malachite, lapis lazuli, rock crystal, or coral, ivory, and pearls, were combined with emeralds, sapphires, rubies and diamonds. Platinum prevailed, although yellow gold still retained an important role and nonprecious metals were not disdained.

The major Parisian *maisons* complemented women's wear with various types of jeweled accessories: toilet cases, lipstick holders, powder compacts, and cigarette holders and cases. For those who, in the era of crazy geometric patterns, still preferred figurative designs, it was possible to choose from among panthers, chimeras, birds, or even floral compositions, interpreted in a new way. The cuts and settings had undergone considerable changes: *baguettes* and squares, with invisible mounts (a technique developed by Claude Arpels and Cartier in the early thirties). The surfaces of the metals, smooth or with a satin finish, permitted sharp or unexpected reflections of light. The illusionistic iridescences favored by art nouveau jewelry vanished. Cartier had been proposing designs of a geometric type since at least 1906, giving a rectilinear form to the traditional garland compositions. The patterns, once stylized, gave rise to forms that, although symmetrical, were completely new and extremely elegant, such as the fountain motif. These designs were first used in small pieces of jewelry like pendants and tie pins, but by 1920 there was a whole collection in the deco style: necklaces of black silk with pendants of pearl tassels, pieces of coral, or *cabochon* stones, or necklaces made up of cylindrical elements, rigid circular bracelets, and earrings with long pendants, cascades of *cabochon* gems, or in circles. The brooches and pins used as ornaments for every accessory, from belts to shoes and hats, or as shoulder decorations for clothes, were sometimes based on Merovingian examples, carefully studied by Cartier's designers. Some were given the structure of miniature works of architecture, in keeping with the decorative repertories adopted in clothing, such as Brialix's afternoon dress, presented in the magazine *Art, Goût, Beauté* in April 1928 and made out of fabric with a design based on the skyscrapers of New York.

The Paris exhibition of 1925 gave a clear picture of the new trends in jewelry. Georges Fouquet was president of the goldsmith's section and the book that he brought out after the exhibition, *La bijouterie et la joaillerie, la bijouterie fantaisie au XXème siècle*, constitutes an invaluable record of the production at that time. In those years Fouquet himself was making jewelry of Oriental inspiration, like the dress ornament in the shape of a Chinese mask, made out of jade and outlined with diamonds, with eyes and hair of onyx,[19] or the oval brooch designed by A. Levillé, again in the shape of a mask, but this time in the African style (Paris, Musée des Arts Décoratifs, Archives Fouquet).[20]

In the thirties, instead of the contrasting colors typical of a popular exotic style of jewelry, he offered the *note blanche* of a combination of platinum and diamonds. As far as the geometric genre was concerned, his creations could attain to an extreme degree of rigor, as in the later brooch (1936-37) designed by Lambert Rucki. Made out of yellow gold, it was triangular in shape, with a smooth surface to which a sphere was attached (Paris, Musée des Arts Décoratifs).

Jean Fouquet, author of the book *Bijoux et Orfèvrerie* published in 1931, first came onto the scene in 1925. Producing designs for jewelry in a geometric style, his reputation was established by the 1937 exhibition.

Evelyn Walsh McLean with the Star of the East diamond mounted on her aigrette, *and the Hope Diamond as a pendant.*

Maria of Serbia with diadem and sautoir of emeralds by Cartier, 1923.

In 1925 Lucien Hirtz had designed a brooch and breast ornament for Boucheron made out of lapis lazuli, jade, coral, onyx, and turquoise. The geometric pattern is influenced by African motifs and is made up of a mosaic of the above stones, outlined by a continuous row of small diamonds (Boucheron Collection).[21]

At the 1925 exhibition Henri Vever presented bracelets designed by Jules Chadel and a series of jewels inspired by Persian miniatures.

Thanks to the innovative character of its products, the firm of Van Cleef & Arpels, founded in 1906 on the basis of an accord between Alfred van Cleef and Charles and Julien Arpels, soon earned itself a place among the major Parisian jewelers that had been in existence since the previous century.[22] Having received an award at the 1925 exhibition for a bracelet of rose-cut rubies, emeralds, and diamonds, the Maison experimented with new techniques, perfecting that of the invisible setting, and created accessories of various types, such as watches or the precious *nécessaires*, a line of compacts and cases in gold, decorated with valuable lacquers and with numerous compartments inside to hold cosmetics and cigarettes, or even an extractable watch. In the twenties the firm brought out a line of products inspired by Indian, Egyptian, Persian, and Chinese forms and decorations.

In the thirties naturalistic subjects were common, playing on the contrast between diamond and brightly colored stones like rubies, emeralds, and sapphires; the metal of choice was platinum. At the end of the thirties there was a return to yellow gold, which was to hold undisputed sway during the following decade. Toward the end of the decade *passe-partout* clips appeared. These could be worn by themselves or hooked up to a serpent's tail necklace. The novelty of convertible jewelry, such as a necklace that turned into a bracelet or a large clip that could be split into two smaller ones, gained Van Cleef & Arpels some very famous clients.

One of the most determined champions of the geometrical style was Raymond Templier (1891-1968) who, after a period of studies at the Ecole des Beaux-Arts, began to work with his father in 1912. From 1929 onward he made use of M. Percheron as his designer. His jewelry offered a rigorous interpretation of functionalist design: schematic and essential, its ornamental solutions were based on a balanced use of materials (precious and not): platinum, diamonds, aquamarines, and black lacquer were the favorites. Templier's reputation was established in Great Britain by the London gallery of the American photographer Curtis Moffat, which sold his creations. The production of Fulco di Verdura (1898-1978), one of the outstanding personalities of the new generation of jewelers, was distinguished by its strong emphasis on color. Verdura, a member of an aristocratic family from Sicily, had initially worked in Paris for Coco Chanel, in 1926, as a fabric designer, but he was then given the job of modifying the splendid jewelry given to the stylist by the Duke of Westminster and the Russian Grand Duke Dmitri. Over the following years Verdura made his celebrated series of Maltese crosses for Coco, out of yellow gold with a myriad of colored stones and used as brooches or earrings, or fixed onto large, rigid bracelets.

While Paris was still the mecca of the world's most chic clientele, there were a large number of German jewelers who had absorbed the ideas of the Bauhaus and used them in a versatile production that was aimed at a broad section of the public. As a consequence they employed an unlimited range of non-precious materials, making no attempt to imitate high-class jewelry but setting out to create "functional pieces of jewelry, that do not conceal their origin."[23] In Austria a multitude of designers, goldsmiths, and silversmiths gathered around the Wiener Werkstätte, active between 1903 and 1913. They took the rigor of the Empire and Biedermeier styles and tried to reconcile it with the influence of Japanese art: the result was the emergence of an independent style, no longer subordinate to the fashions set by France. In Italy the engraver and goldsmith Dario Viterbo (1890-1961), who worked in Florence and Paris, adopted the deco style, achieving considerable success at the Monza Biennale in 1923. Giacomo and Alfredo Ravasco followed the same trend, and this change in style, particularly in the work of Alfredo, was evident at the Monza Biennali and the Paris exhibition of 1925.

The economic crisis of 1929, even though fashion designers attempted to

Jean Fouquet, Necklace in gold, platinum, black lacquer, and aquamarine, 1925-30. Private Collection.

Fulco di Verdura, Ivory bracelets with Maltese crosses in gold, pearls, brilliants, sapphires, and rubies.

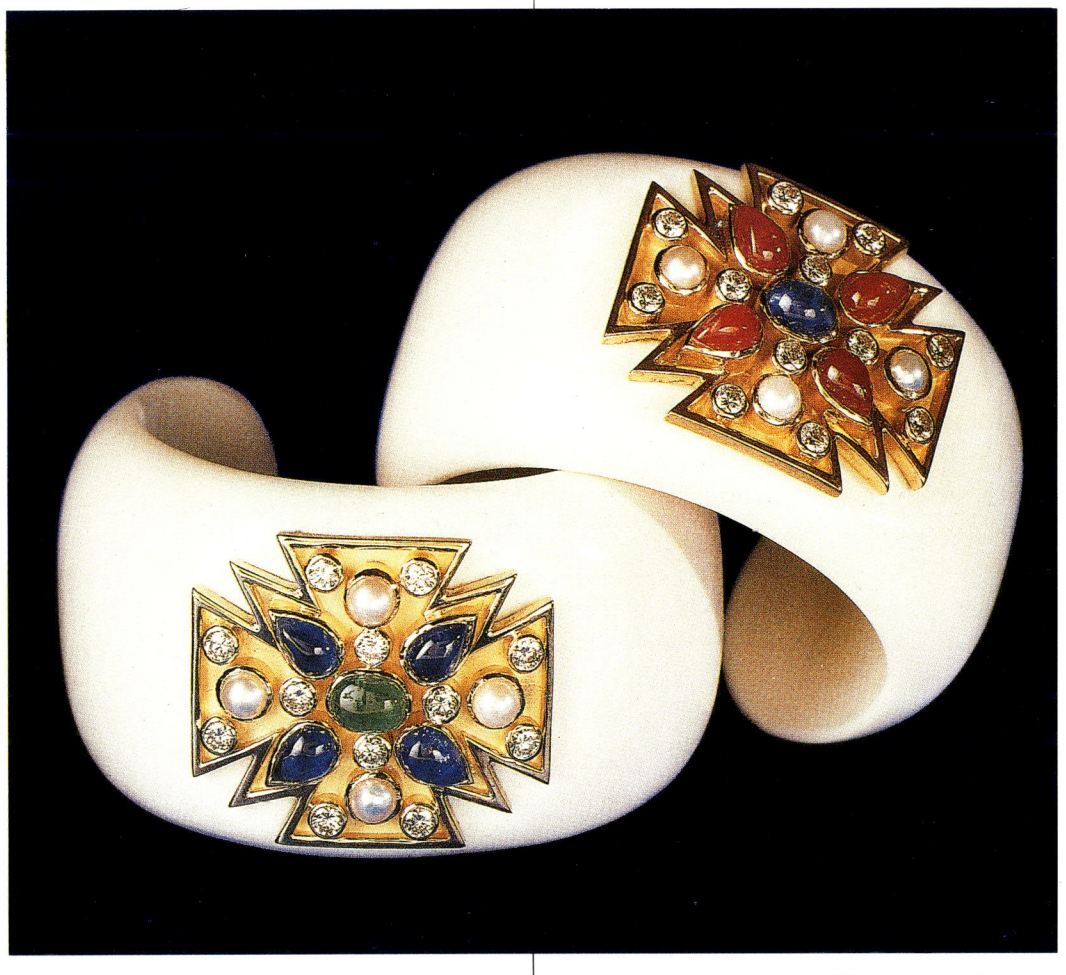

exorcise it with a line of flowing and draped garments (long dresses, in contrast to the short hemlines of the previous decade, and crosscut fabric meant higher costs for materials), proved the German producers right.

In the world of high-class jewelry the effects of a worldwide slump on such a scale were hard to check. American clients were growing more scarce and many Parisian workshops shifted to the production of costume jewelry. René Lalique, for example, began to experiment with glass, and even in this sector there was a move from more expensive hand-crafted objects to mass production, on an industrial scale. Bakelite, which had already found a place in cheap jewelry after the First World War, came fully into its own with the crash of 1929 and odd and brightly colored jewelry from America invaded the department stores, competing with European manufacturers.[24]

Further exotic influences came from the colonial exhibition held in Vincennes in 1931: the plants and animals of the French colonies were taken up by jewelers, who in earlier decades had already created pieces in the shape of elephants, panthers, leopards, and tigers. In Paris the panther *par excellence* was Jeanne Toussaint, close friend and inseparable collaborator of Louis Cartier for a lifetime. Her apt nickname, indicative of a powerful character or even of her life style, was linked with a popular line of Cartier jewelry and objects, inaugurated by Pierre in 1915 with the panther he gave to his wife. The tradition continued over the following decade, with some absolutely original and refined results, such as the famous panther on a large *cabochon* sapphire made for the Duchess of Windsor, in 1948 (plate 113).

At the Paris exhibition of 1937 both high-class jewelry and costume jewelry displayed a softening of geometric forms, with curved lines predominat-

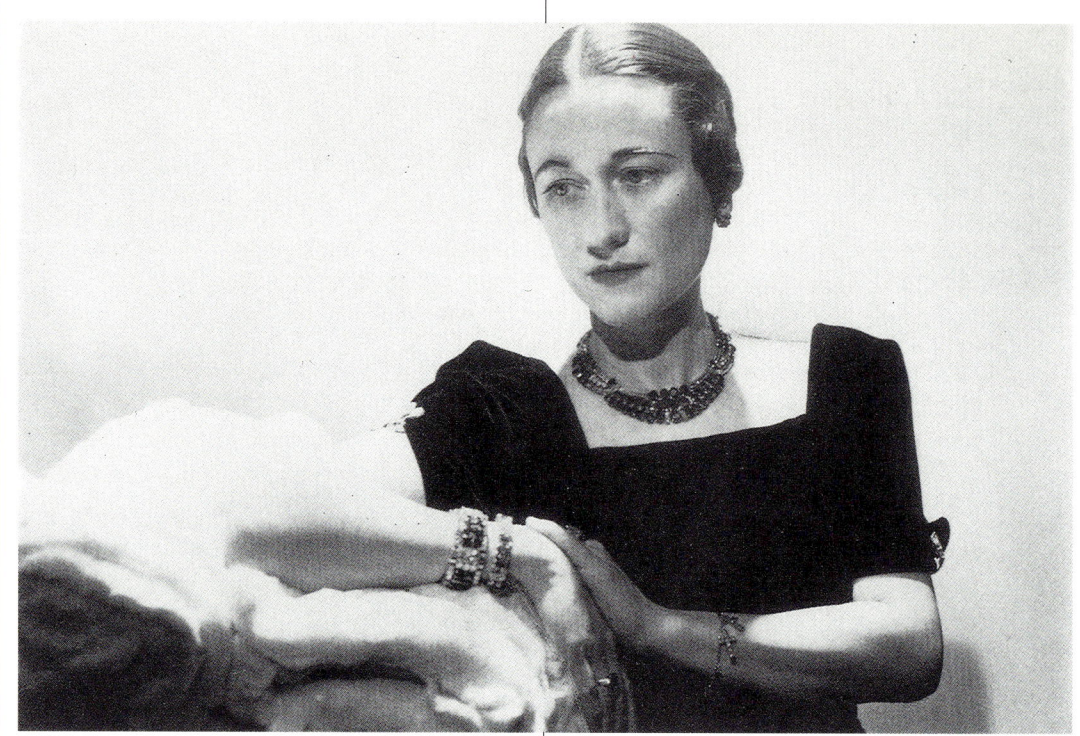

Group of rings in yellow gold, brilliants, pearl, and carved jade, 1940-50. Private Collection.

ing over straight ones and naturalistic themes reemerging: the general shift toward sculptural values rather than architectural ones marked the decline of the deco style and the beginning of a new phase in the aesthetics of jewelry.

Caprices of Form

Toward the end of the thirties, while French production, which dominated international fashion, seemed to stagnate, unable to make a creative leap beyond the somewhat mellowed schemes of deco jewelry, the unbridled imagination of the movie world of Hollywood was beginning to have an effect. An Austrian jeweler, though he went by the name of Joseff of Hollywood, had rendered immortal the faces and *décolletés* of many stars, including Greta Garbo, Marlene Dietrich, Vivien Leigh, and Bette Davis, as they shifted flexibly from one historic role to another. Marcel Boucher and Trifari had also been among the major suppliers of this great dream factory.[25]

Equally spectacular pieces of stage jewelry made in Italy for the stars of opera have not achieved the same legendary fame, even though a recently complet-

Wallis Simpson in a photograph taken by Cecil Beaton in 1936, with the necklace by Van Cleef & Arpels that was modified in 1939 by the addition of a cascade of rubies. The necklace is dated and inscribed: "My Wallis from her David 19.VI.36".

ed examination of these pieces attests to their fascination and quality, showing that they have every right to be counted among the masterpieces of twentieth-century jewelry.[26]

The revival of past styles sparked off by reconstructions of history in movies during the thirties and forties was also reflected in the design of cheap jewelry for the general public, although the fantasy of American designers was not held in check by considerations of philological accuracy. Absolutely unprecedented solutions emerged from the vast range of costume jewelry that, as a result of the ban on the use of metals during the war, experimented with a wide variety of alternative materials (Bakelite, wood, plaster, leather).

The large diamond necklace that Barbara Hutton purchased from Cartier in 1939 was perhaps one of the last contacts between European jewelers and American customers before the war brought a halt to trade. The absence of models imposed on the international market by the great Parisian houses allowed American designers to give free rein to their imagination. Their inventions drew on a multitude of ideas derived from the traditional cultures of United States, as well as on the glittering, vacuous world of the cinema.

The emphasis was on opulent adornment, spectacular invention, unusual color contrasts, strange and provocative subjects, as well, in the more traditional type of jewelry based on flowers and animals, as designs that appeared to have no possible connection with those of the past. The American style had developed out of ostentatious transgression of the canons of European culture, finding expression, in the realm of architecture for instance, in the "crazy houses" of California. These were large inhabitable sculptures representing animals or everyday objects: a gigantic flower vase was considered the ideal premises for a florist, or an enormous dog for a hot-dog stand.[27]

So, in the realm of jewelry, anything became possible: the body of a deer could be formed out of many flowers of faceted crystal, a winged putto with green crystals mounted on its wings might use three chains to pull a cloud with crystal stars (and be used as a brooch), two pen nibs could be turned into clips, while a large bracelet might be decorated with wedding scenes.[28] An emphasis on bright colors and a passion for nature distinguished the creations of Fulco di Verdura, who had moved to New York in 1939. The Maltese crosses he had designed for Coco Chanel were still highly popular and he continued to invent variations on this medieval theme, such as the platinum and diamond brooch he made for the actress Pola Negri in 1940. Although he had been one of the first to return to the use of yellow gold, he also produced many pieces in platinum, diamonds, and pearls. In the brooch in the shape of two masks facing one another, made for Clare Boothe Luce in 1940 in celebration of her performance in *The Women*, he used both metals, together with sapphires, emeralds, diamonds, and pearls. On the oth-

Van Cleef & Arpels, Zip necklace, in gold and diamonds; can be closed to form a bracelet, circa 1950.

er hand, he avoided contrasting colors in another splendid brooch, dating from 1946. Completely white, it is made up of two wings studded with diamonds and a large pendent pearl. But there was one particular type of ornament that fascinated the most enthusiastic collectors of jewelry, such as the Duchess of Windsor: that of the brooch in the form of a shell made of yellow gold and decorated with stones like sapphires and diamonds (plate 143). In these shells Verdura revealed the most direct link with his native Sicily, and he showed incomparable mastery in his use of them in high-class jewelry, compacts, for instance, made out of the two valves of a large shell, mounted with a network of knotted ropes in yellow gold (one of the motifs most widely imitated in necklaces and bracelets) and with a clasp made of a white pearl and a black pearl.

For the more important occasions, such as anniversaries and the opening nights of theaters and nightclubs, it was *de rigeur* for members of New York high society to wear Verdura's creations. His collaboration with Salvador Dalí opened up new possibilities for expression for his already fertile creativity: "Fulco and I have tried to find out whether jewelry was made for painting or painting for jewelry. We are sure, however, that they are made for one another," declared Dalí in an aphorism published by *Vogue* in July 1941. The happy marriage between the two artists spread the fame of the aristocratic creator of jewelry beyond the confines of an élite circle of clients.

Other European craftsmen chose to go to the United States. In 1940 Jean Schlumberger moved from Paris to New York, where he collaborated with Nicholas Bongard. "I observe nature and find verve," he declared: sea horses, flowers, fish, birds, and angels are the most frequent subjects of his intricate and lively jewelry, in which he

Queen Elizabeth of England, in 1951, with a tiara of diamonds by Cartier.

The Queen Mother of England wearing a diadem of diamonds made by Cartier in 1953.

used colored stones and enamel. His collaboration with Tiffany resulted in an updating of the firm's design.

Animals were also the inspiration for the sculptural and bizarre jewelry of David Webb, who was active in New York from the forties onward, together with Nina Silberstein.

When, after the end of the war, the production of high-class jewelry began to revive in Europe, the legacy of the American costume jewelry of the wartime period could clearly be seen, though in its proportions rather than in the eccentricity of its designs.

The precious jewelry of the forties was characterized by a showy plasticism, although the massive, rounded, twisted, and knotted forms were not in fact as heavy as they looked, since most of the pieces were hollow inside.[29] Gold held undisputed sway, although white metals and stones—diamond along with the whole gamut of precious and semiprecious stones—lent a touch of the picturesque to these miniature works of sculpture, with their soft, solid, and rotund forms, so similar to the canons of beauty for the ideal woman of the time, whose Junoesque and soldierly charms were emphasized by the large padded shoulders of their clothes and their sculptural, orthopedic shoes with high cork heels.

Asymmetrical bows, knots, drapery, and fan-shaped motifs were the most common elements of brooches and earrings that looked as if they had been molded out of clay. Alongside sinuous outlines for clasps and rings, there was a preference for grating effects and openwork resembling lace, supple meshes made up of polygonal elements and used in large band-like bracelets, or slippery rattail or gas-tube necklaces. A series of fundamental changes within Maison Cartier date from the forties. In 1942 Jacques and Louis died. Jeanne Toussaint and Pierre remained in charge of the empire, supported by

Louis's son Claude and by Jean-Jacques. Peter Lemarchand became the new designer, concentrating his attention on reworking one of the Maison's favorite themes, the panther. In tune with the ornamental style of the moment, his new line of panthers took on a sculptural and naturalistic character. The most famous example is undoubtedly the one made for the Duchess of Windsor in 1948. Wallis adored the animal models of the Parisian house and considered her brooch in the shape of a flamingo, dating from 1940, to be a genuine lucky charm. She was also proud of the impression that the jewel had created among journalists, on her arrival in Miami with Edward in 1941. Even the lorgnette with its precious handle in the shape of a tiger, made of gold with black enamel and emeralds, was destined to go down in history: René Boyché depicted them in the portrait of the duchess "with the tiger-lorgnette-Cartier" published by *Vogue America* in May 1953.[30]

For Van Cleef & Arpels as well the decade from 1930 to 1940 saw the emergence of the second generation. The firm expanded, setting up branches in Japan and the United States. The creations of the previous decade became the classics of the house, which supplied the outstanding personalities of the entertainment and aristocratic world: *passe-partout* brooches, matched with serpent's tail necklaces, and "ludo" bracelets, the first example of which dates from 1934 and had been given this name in honor of Louis Arpels, who was known as Ludovico (plate 36). These last are composed of broad jointed bands, made up of polygonal elements and have a precious fastening set with gems. The floral or animal motifs made by the technique of invisible setting were joined by another model destined to become a classic: that of the ballerina. At the beginning of the forties, after its success at the New York exhibition of 1939, the firm conquered America, and from that time on the list of its illustrious clients grew rapidly: the Kennedys and Vanderbilts, Gloria Swanson, the Aga Khan, King Farouk, and Marlene Dietrich were just some of its regular customers.

Elizabeth Taylor with a tiara of pearls, diamonds, and brilliants made by Van Cleef & Arpels.

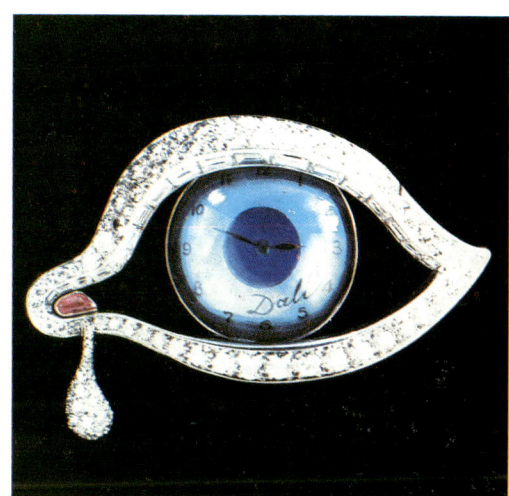
Salvador Dalí, "Time's Eye" watch, enameled platinum and diamonds. New York, Oven Cheaton Foundation.

Diamonds Are a Girl's Best Friend
"Diamonds are a girl's best friend," sang Marilyn Monroe, confident of summing up the aspirations, as far as jewelry was concerned, of the elegant woman of the fifties.

The distinction between costume jewelry and precious jewelry, which had grown blurred at times in previous decades, owing to the frequent use of semiprecious materials in both sectors, became marked again in the years of the postwar economic recovery. It now became possible to distinguish a number of distinct tendencies in jewelry. The important piece to be worn on grand occasions, for which platinum and diamonds came back into vogue, along with the whole range of gemstones (ruby, sapphire, emerald), bore the trademark of the major firms, as far as both design and execution were concerned.

Another, but less demanding type of jewelry, on the economic plane as well, though one that was still made out of precious materials, was that linked to a sort of mass production. As a result of the industrial development of the sector, this kind of jewelry was becoming increasingly common throughout Europe. In Italy places like Valenza or Arezzo, where there was an ancient tradition of goldsmithery, became the main centers for this mass production. The number of small and medium-sized industries producing precious ornaments increased at a dizzy pace, to meet a demand that was growing in parallel with the rapid economic development of the fifties. The genre of the precious ornament also became a field of experimentation for some of the greatest artists of the time, who recognized that jewelry and gold had an expressive value of their own, on a par with that of great sculpture.

Even on the front of costume jewelry, the range of production was growing increasingly diverse, and there were at least three levels of quality. Elegant but rather nonconformist women were able to appreciate the creativity of the *bijou de couture*, and to alternate it indiscriminately with expensive parures. In any case large numbers of people preferred to buy mass-produced jewelry, though made out of precious metal.

In the enthusiasm of the economic recovery, new centers of style were emerging to challenge the monopoly of French fashion. In Florence, in 1951, Giovanni Battista Giorgini launched "made in Italy" fashion, exploiting the fascination and aristocratic-provincial setting of the city that had been the cradle of European art. The city has always had a special place in the American imagination, and it was this chord that the clothes Giorgini put on show were intended to strike. Italian stylists demonstrated their professionalism and good taste, and Parisian *haute couture*, with its already well established names, was now faced with a far from negligible rival.[31]

The same phenomenon occurred in the world of jewelry, which saw the major Italian designers come to the forefront of the international market.

With the third generation of the Bulgari dynasty, jewelers of Greek origin who had moved to Rome at the end of the nineteenth century, the firm developed a stylistic profile of its own. Its production was characterized by the use of colored gemstones cut *en cabochon* and surrounded by *baguette* diamonds in bracelets, necklaces, and rings. Another well-known feature was the reference to antiquity, with the insertion of Greek, Etruscan, and Roman

Gold brooch designed by Pablo Picasso and made by François Hugo. Paris, Galerie Le Point-Cardinal.

Georges Braque, Brooch in gold, diamonds, and jasper, inspired by the return of Icarus to Sparta. London, Gimpels Fils.

coins found in archeological excavations into soft and wide bracelets. Evidence for the fact that jewelry "made in Italy" had succeeded in winning over the American public comes from a remark made by Andy Warhol, who declared, not without a touch of irony, that he always went to Bulgari's on his visits to Rome, as it was the most important museum of contemporary art.[32]

In the same years the creations of Faraone, who had moved from Naples to Milan after the First World War, Cusi in Milan, Fasano in Turin, Fecarotta in Catania, Settepassi and Enrico Serafini in Florence, Uno a Erre in Arezzo, Missaglia in Venice, and Illario in Valenza all acquired an international reputation.

A look at the models most in vogue in the fifties reveals the importance of jewelry to be worn around the neck, which was well suited to the low-cut dresses of the time. The meshwork types of the previous decade remained popular, but were joined by an endless range of models.[33] A sure grasp of technique brought out the potential of the materials, giving rise to a wide variety of objects: smooth or twisted threads of gold, tubular meshes, plaitwork resembling woven fabric, braids, herringbone patterns, cords, beads, leaves, spirals, fringes, nets, and sunbursts. The combination with gemstones was equally varied: pendants of diamond, emerald, ruby, or sapphire. Naturalistic motifs were arranged along the edges of broad necklaces or hung down asymmetrically. Even tie- or collar-shaped models were studded with stones. One of the most original creations was the necklace-scarf designed by Jean Cocteau for Boucheron, made out of gold worked to create the effect of tulle and edged with rubies. Van Cleef & Arpels also came up with an original design in the *fermeture éclair* necklace, in the form of a working zip, which could be worn as a bracelet when closed.

The variety of forms and combinations of gems was equally great in the pendants for earrings. The old Parisian firm of Mellerio dit Meller, which had gone back to making its own jewelry in the forties, proposed a series of interesting designs for earrings, such as the one with a cascade of brilliants set in a spiral motif of gold wire, with a large rectangular topaz pendant. Brooches were the most common accessories, again with an extremely large repertory of designs, ranging from animals to flowers. The great variety of interpretations and goldworking techniques included single leaves, floral compositions, and feathers, made out of gold wire and studded with gemstones, birds, and insects, as well as cascades of round and *baguette* brilliants. The idea of the ruby and diamond brooch in the form of a palm, designed by Georges Rémy for Cartier in 1957, represented one of the most original alternatives to the standard naturalistic motifs.

Mesh and braid patterns were also to be found in rings, which were generally fairly rounded and with a large central stone framed by circles of smaller gems. But there were also patterns with knots and asymmetrical interlacery. The pompon motif, invented by the Mellerio firm, remains one of the most bizarre: a raised central stone is surrounded by a sort of fringe that gives the design its name. All the types of meshwork tried out in necklaces were also used for bracelets: Cartier also produced *torchons* or plaits composed of gold spheres and the classic types derived from the garland style were common as well, and usually made out of platinum and diamonds. Around 1955 woven designs came into vogue, of the cuff type or with rigid and rounded forms, and wristwatches were transformed into elegant bracelets studded with gems.

Although semiprecious stones were not particularly common, amethyst, opal, and topaz were used, along with coral and turquoise. In 1957 Cartier produced a brooch in the form of a Moor's head, made of tortoiseshell, with collar, turban, and aigrette in gold, diamond, and turquoise.

With the preference for white that was characteristic of the jewelry of these years, pearls came back into the limelight again and became a synonym for *charme* and elegance. Prince Ranier of Monaco acquired a parure of pearls and diamonds from Van Cleef & Arpels for Princess Grace in 1957. More famous than these, however, are the pearls he bought from Cartier at the time of his marriage, after an international scandal had flared up over his earlier purchase of another necklace, from another Parisian jeweler.[34]

In aristocratic circles, receptions and anniversaries still presented an opportunity for the display of head ornaments and the diadem remained a symbol of social distinction. Cartier produced necklaces that could be converted into tiaras, for those who did not

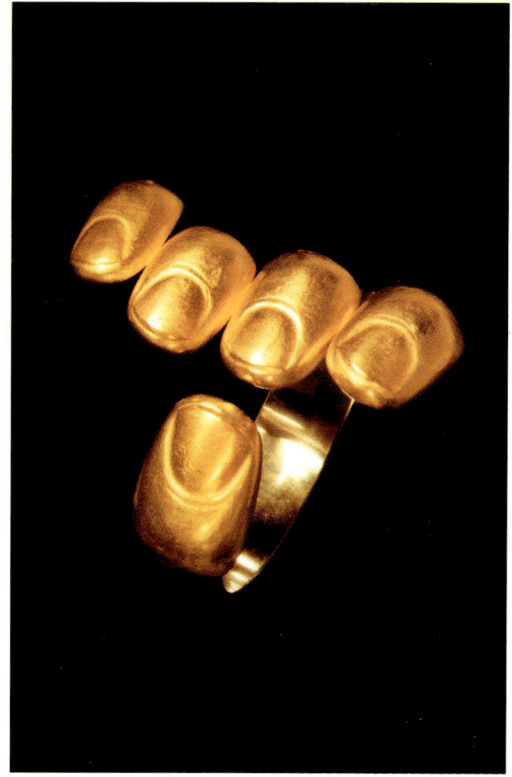

Bruno Martinazzi, "Goldfinger" bracelet, in yellow and white gold. (Photo Martinazzi)

Bruno Martinazzi, "Hand" brooch in gold. (Photo Martinazzi)

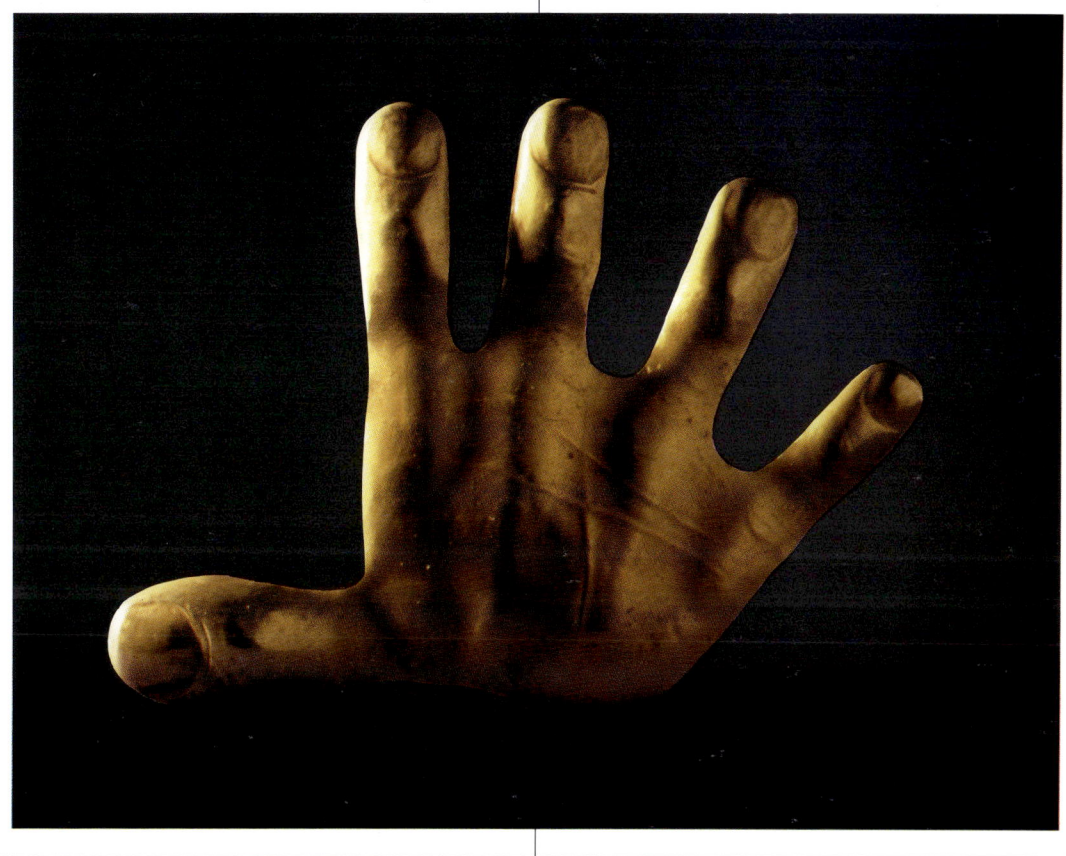

possess one among the family jewels. The coronation of Elizabeth II in 1953 made the need for a new decoration of this type impelling, and the London goldsmith Mew created a new diadem of diamonds for the Queen Mother. The marriage of Grace Kelly and Ranier required the same kind of jewelry and Aristotle Onassis gave the splendid bride a tiara of platinum, brilliants, and *cabochon* rubies purchased from Cartier. In the movie and entertainment world too there was emulation of important jewelry, with an aristocratic tone. Outstanding among the rich and bejeweled actresses was Elizabeth Taylor who, among other things, flaunted a diadem with pearls, diamonds, and brilliants made by Van Cleef & Arpels. Maria Callas too, at the peak of her success, showed a preference for extravagant and classic sets of diamonds.

So the prevailing taste of the decade was one linked to the themes of traditional jewelry. The creative efforts of designers succeeded in producing an infinite variety of solutions, but all based on the stock motifs of the naturalistic repertory or on those of knots, cascades, and tassels. On the technical plane, on the other hand, it was the materials that held absolute sway, with virtuoso effects obtained through the working of gold and platinum, molded to resemble textiles or ribbons of cloth. A confident mastery of techniques and a tone of opulence sought through the ostentation of gemstones were the distinctive characteristics of jewelry in the fifties.

Transformations in Taste and Significance
On his election to the Académie Française in 1955, Jean Cocteau (1889-1963) designed the hilt of his own sword, which was made for him by Cartier. The hilt is in the form of the poet's own profile bound to a column with a ribbon, surmounted by a lyre (to symbolize the theater and his literary activity),

Arnaldo Pomodoro, Necklace in gold and precious stones.

Bruno Martinazzi, "Apple" ring in yellow and white

while at the base are represented two pencils in reference to his parallel activity as a graphic artist.[35]

The poet and artist had showed a marked interest in the genre of jewelry on more than one occasion, as found in the above-mentioned necklace-scarf he designed for Boucheron, made out of gold tulle, with rubies and a turquoise as a clasp.

In itself, the fact could be dismissed as the eccentricity of an intellectual, but in a broader context it is revealed as a symptom of a tendency that was destined to dominate the production of the following decade.

In the world of costume jewelry the figure of the designer began to overshadow that of the manufacturers, with the result that firms tried to get famous personalities from the art and fashion worlds to design their jewelry. So the foundations for a renewal were sought in the trends of avant-garde art, as is suggested by a statement made by Paco Rabanne: "I wanted to create jewelry that would recall the paintings of that period, extravagant, crazy, and uninhibited."[36]

If fashion designers in the sixties looked to the world of the "fine arts," the interest was in fact reciprocated. Although a vast range of expensive jewelry remained conditioned by certain conventions of the sophisticated "look," the work of many artists shows, from the fifties onward, a rediscovery of the possibilities of expression inherent in the ornament.

Jewelry became a field of experimentation: painters devoted themselves to the renewal of its design, drawing primarily on the ideas of the avant-garde movements; in the same way sculptors sought to exploit the expressive capacities of metals and gemstones, creating irregular and bizarre forms that in some cases emphasized the characteristics of the raw material, with surprising luministic effects.

Out of this developed the genre of artist's jewelry, of the one-off piece, which treated the ornament more as an object to be looked at than as something to be worn and that, in the same way as a painting or a work of sculpture, could communicate the feelings of its creator. This was the intention of Salvador Dalí when, in 1954, he exhibited a collection of his jewelry at the Bernheim Jeune Gallery in New York: "They have been created to delight the eyes, to elevate the spirit, to stimulate the imagination, to make condemnations. Without an audience, without the presence of spectators, they would not be able to fulfill the function for which they have been created. So the spectator becomes the principal artist: his vision, his heart, his mind come together in the attempt to grasp the intention of the person who has created them, and bring them to life."

François Hugo had been the interpreter and executor of jewelry designed by Jean Cocteau, Max Ernst, and Pablo Picasso, but ventures into the field of jewelry can be found in the work of other artists. Man Ray, for example, designed a brooch of gold and lapis lazuli, in the form of a portrait in profile. The same taste for the combination of precious metals and gemstones with elements made of semiprecious stones is characteristic of the jewelry designed by Georges Braque and exhibited in Paris in 1963. The group, consisting of more than a hundred pieces, was based on themes drawn from ancient mythology. As far back as the end of the thirties, the American sculptor Alexander Calder (1898-1976) had applied the experiments he had made in the realm of abstract sculpture to jewelry. The pieces were made out of brass wire and animated, like his celebrated mobiles, by ingenious tricks.

Over the course of the fifties, however, there were numerous sculptors who applied their creative talents to various types of ornament.

Giacomo Manzù, Gold brooch in the form of a dove, 1968. Ardea, Raccolta Manzù.

Giacomo Manzù, Brooch in the form of a feather in gold, brilliants, and emeralds, 1969. Ardea, Raccolta Manzù.

For Arnaldo and Giò Pomodoro the making of jewelry constituted the initial and trial phase for formal designs that would later find expression in large-scale works of sculpture. Yet Arnaldo Pomodoro, referring to his "work for new jewelry" around the middle of the fifties, attributed a number of specific aims of renewal to this aspect of his activity: "While in art the contemporary period, from the mid-nineteenth century to the present, has constituted a true revolution in aesthetics with respect to tradition, in the so-called minor arts this has not happened except in exceptional cases. So for me it was a question of bringing about a transformation in taste and significance."[37]

Ever since the middle of the fifties, the sculptor Bruno Martinazzi has devoted much of his artistic activity to goldsmithery: he takes the inspiration for his jewelry from the world of nature, or represents parts of the human body such as the eyes, lips, and fingers, combining different-colored layers of gold and platinum.[38]

The first international exhibition of modern jewelry, held in London in 1961, was able to show just how wide-

spread the phenomenon of the production of original handcrafted jewelry had become.

The event provided an opportunity for craftsmen of different nationalities to compare their work and presented a spectacular range of creations that offered real possibilities for a renewal of the art of jewelry. The dominant characteristic was that of experimentation with textures, with forms growing increasingly abstract and free from the conditioning of the traditional themes of jewelry. Attention was drawn to the qualities of the material through daring effects of irregularity; surfaces were rough, wrinkled as the bark of a tree. In other cases, however, the emphasis was on severe and complex geometrical patterns or on linear and bizarre forms derived from the use of gold and silver wire.

The pieces of jewelry produced by Flora Wiechmann Savioli were also made up of dense tangles of spirals and thin corrugated sheets of metal. In the work of Giacomo Manzù, on the other hand, we find a return to more traditional figurative themes. He took animals as the subjects for his jewelry, creating gold brooches in the shape of a dove, a dormouse, a turtle eating a snake, or a feather embellished with an emerald and diamonds.

The evolution of artist's jewelry followed a separate route from that of high-class jewelry but had a more direct influence on the production of costume jewelry. The craft revival of the late sixties turned the interest of many young people in this direction. In 1972 the Artwear gallery in New York sold jewelry designed by the greatest artists of the day as well as jewelry made by unknown craftsmen, presenting them as works of art.[39]

The creations of high-class jewelry, on the other hand, encountered much more difficulty in renewing themselves. Although updated, the repertory of forms already amply tried out over previous decades remained essentially the same. Animals and flowers were the dominant themes. David Webb set the trend in this area and the creations of Fulco di Verdura were among the most innovative.

The piece of jewelry that revealed a mastery of technique and flashed with precious stones had not lost its fascination, and this was demonstrated by the fact that during the sixties the market for antique and precious diamonds or sapphires acquired some celebrated customers.

Among the surviving great Parisian houses, Van Cleef & Arpels remained one of the most important points of reference for the world's aristocracy. The Shah of Iran commissioned new jewels to add to the spectacular ones in his crown. In 1967 Barbara Hutton acquired a tiara with pearls and diamonds.

Cartier, on the other hand, closed its New York store in 1962. Within the space of a few years the house's production was reorganized by Robert Hocq, Joseph Kanoui, and Alain Perrin. In 1973 they set up a sales network on a large-scale, distributed through franchises located all over the world: this was the era of *Les must de Cartier*: the objects, watches, and jewelry of the Parisian Maison once again became the models for a lucrative trade in fakes.

Within the space of a few years the production of the great jewelers of the first half of the century has come to be seen as a fundamental chapter in the history of jewelry. Today the taste and technical skill of the pieces realized during this period fascinate the most exclusive and refined of collectors: it is their "style" that has left an indelible mark on the "extraordinary jewelry" produced from the era of art nouveau up to the sixties and that ensures that it will never fade, however much fashions change.

[1] Cf. Marquardt 1989.
[2] On the production of Castellani, cf. Munn 1983, Snowman 1990, pp. 9-28.
[3] On this subject, cf. Schmuck 1989, p. 56.
[4] Cf. Nadelhoffer 1984, p. 87.
[5] *Ibidem*, pp. 45-65.
[6] Cf. Koechert 1990, p. 86.
[7] On Vever cf. in particular, Snowman 1990, pp. 143 and 154.
[8] On this type, cf. Nadelhoffer 1984, p. 87.
[9] On the goldsmith's activity, cf. Falk 1985; Schmuck 1989, pp. 158-166.
[10] For a complete treatment of the artist's work, cf. Becker 1987; Waller 1988; Schmuck 1989, pp. 214-231; Mortimer 1989.
[11] Cf. Becker 1989, pp. 17-46.
[12] Cf. Schmuck 1989, p. 141.
[13] On Boucheron production, cf. *130 Années de Création*, 1988; Schmuck 1989, pp. 132-152, with previous bibliography.
[14] *Ornament und verbrechen*, 1908.
[15] On the fashion of these years, cf. *Anni venti...*, 1992.
[16] On Erté's designs, from which precious pieces of jewelry were made, cf. *Erté...*, 1991.
[17] Cf. Paolieri, "Amore senz'ali," in *Lidel*, November 15, 1926, p. 97.
[18] Cf. Edizioni Mondadori, 1981, p. 128.
[19] Cf. Snowman 1990, p. 166.
[20] *Ibidem*, p. 84.
[21] *Ibidem*, p. 171.
[22] On the production of Van Cleef & Arpels, cf. the recent exhibition catalogue.
[23] Cf. *I gioielli della fantasia...*, 1991, p. 77. With regard to German production, cf. the detailed repertories of Weber 1989 and Fahrner 1990.
[24] On the production of costume jewelry in America, cf. D. Farneti Cera, "Il lusso della libertà, la libertà del lusso," in *I gioielli della fantasia...*, 1991, pp. 149-221; on Bakelite in particular, cf. Davidov, Redington Dawes 1988.
[25] On this subject the reader is referred to the recent book by Ball, 1991.
[26] Cf. Pennati, Asnicar 1991.
[27] Cf. Heimann 1985.
[28] On this subject, cf. *I gioielli della fantasia...*, 1991, pp. 149-221.
[29] On the production of jewelry in the forties, cf. Gabardi 1989.
[30] Cf. Gautier 1987, p. 236.
[31] On the birth of Italian fashion, cf. *La Sala Bianca...*, 1992.
[32] Cf. Snowman 1990, p. 238.
[33] On the models of jewelry in the fifties, cf. Gabardi 1989.
[34] Cf. Gautier 1987, pp. 231-232.
[35] Cf. Nadelhoffer 1984, p. 148.
[36] Cf. Becker, "Il ritorno dell'ornamento," in *I gioielli della fantasia...*, 1991, pp. 314 and 330.
[37] Cf. *Progettare con l'oro*, 1979, p. 36.
[38] On his production, cf. De Bartolomeis 1977.
[39] Cf. Becker, op. cit., in *I gioielli della fantasia...*, 1991, p. 332.

Essential Bibliography

1908
H. Vever, *La Bijouterie Française au XIX siècle*, 3 vols., Paris 1908.
1973
B. Anderson, *Storia dei gioielli*, Novara 1973.
1975
G. Massobrio, P. Portoghesi, *Album del Liberty*, Bari 1975.
1976
G. Massobrio, P. Portoghesi, *Album degli anni venti*, Bari 1976.
B. Schaukal, *Beitraege zur Wiener Schmuckkunst um 1900 unter besonderer Beruecksichtigung der Wiener Werkstaette*, Vienna 1976.
1977
S. Barten, *René Lalique. Schmuck und Objet d'art 1890-1910*, Munich 1977.
1978
R. Schmutzler, *Art Nouveau*, New York 1978.
1979
E. Charles-Roux, *Le temps Chanel*, Paris 1979.
Progettare con l'oro, exhibition catalogue, Florence 1979.
1980
V. Becker, *Antique and Twentieth Century Jewelry*, London 1980.
1982
M. Gabardi, *Gioielli anni 1940*, Milan 1982.
G. Gautier, *La saga dei Cartier (Rue de la Paix)*, Milan 1982.
T. Menten, *Authentic Art Déco Jewelry Design*, New York 1982.
1983
M.N. Gary, *Les Fouquet, Bijoutiers et Joailliers à Paris 1860-1960*, Paris 1983.
G.C. Munn, *Les Bijoutiers Castellani et Giuliano. Retour à l'antique au XX siècle*, Fribourg 1983.
1984
H. Nadelhoffer, *Cartier, Jewellers Extraordinary*, London 1984.
H. Nadelhoffer, *Cartier*, Paris 1984.
J. Sataloff, *Art Nouveau Jewelry*, Bryn Mawr 1984.
1985
V. Becker, *Art Nouveau Jewelry*, London 1985.
M. Dufrène, *305 Authentic Art Nouveau Jewelry Designs*, New York.
1985
F. Falk, *Europaeischer Schmuck, vom Historismus bis zum Jugendstil Koenisbach-Stein*, Bühl-Baden 1985.
J. Heimann, R. Georges, *California Crazy*, 2nd ed., Tokyo 1985.
S. Raulet, *Art Déco Jewelry*, London 1985.
J. Stancliffe, *Costume and Fashion Jewelry of the Twentieth Century*, London 1985.
1986
B. Cartlidge, *Les Bijoux au XX siècle*, Paris 1986.
M. Gabardi, *Les bijoux de l'Art Déco aux Années '40*, Paris 1986.
Giacomo Manzù, exhibition catalogue, Florence 1986.
S. Roulet, *Van Cleef & Arpels*, New York 1986.
1987
J. Culme, N. Rayner, *The Jewels of the Duchess of Windsor*, New York 1987.
G. Gautier, *La saga dei Cartier*, 2nd ed., Sperling and Kupfer 1987.
1988
I. Becker, *Schmuckkunst im Jugendstil*, Berlin 1988.
Boucheron. 130 années de création et d'emotion, exhibition catalogue, Paris 1988.
I capolavori di Cartier, exhibition catalogue, Naples 1988.
C. Davidov, G. R. Dawes, *The Bakelite Jewelry Book*, New York 1988.
The Jewelry of René Lalique, London 1987.
J. Mulvagh, *Costume Jewelry in Vogue*, London 1988.
H. Nadelhoffer, *Cartier*, Milan 1988.
G. Néret, *Boucheron. Four Generations of a World Renowned Jeweler*, New York 1988.
T. Paul, *Louis Comfort Tiffany*, Novara 1988.
1989
D. Bennet, D. Mascetti, *I gioielli, come riconoscerli e valutarli*, Milan 1989.
M. Gabardi, *Gioielli anni '50*, 2nd ed., Milan 1989.
B. Marquardt, "Bisher unbekannte Zeichnungen angeblich nach Benvenuto Cellini," in *Weltkunst*, 1, 1989, pp. 16-20.
T.L. Mortimer, *Lalique Jewellery and Glassware*, London 1989.
Pariser Schmuck, exhibition catalogue, Munich 1989.
D. Scarisbrick (ed.), *Jewellery, Makers, Motifs, History, Techniques*, London 1989.
H. Tait, *Gioielli 7000 anni di storia*, Milan 1989.
C. Weber, *Schmuck der 20er und 30er Jahre in Deutschland*, Stuttgart 1989.
1990
Var. Authors, *Gioielli, arte e materia*, San Fermo (CO) 1990.
L'arte di Cartier, exhibition catalogue, Italian ed., Bologna 1990.
J. Booth, *L'arte di Fabergé*, Milan 1990.
T. Fahrner, *Scmuck zwischen Avantgard und Tradition*, Stuttgart 1990.
P. Fossati, C.G. Barbisio, *Martinazzi*, Turin 1990.
Gioielli e legature. Artisti del XX secolo, exhibition catalogue, Milan 1990.
I.V. Hauser Koechert, *Imperial Jewellers in Vienna*, Florence 1990.
A. Kenneth Snowman, *The Master Jewelers*, New York 1990.
D. Scarisbrick, *Ancestral Jewels*, New York 1990.
1991
S. Bury, *Jewellery 1789-1910. The International Era*, 2 vols., London 1991.
J. Dubbs Ball, *Jewelry of the Stars, Creations from Joseff of Hollywood*, Westchester 1991.
D. Farneti Cera (ed.), *I gioielli della fantasia. Ornamenti del XX secolo nell'arte, nel costume, nella moda*, Milan 1991.
Marshall Lee (ed.), *Erté Arte da indossare. Gioielli*, Milan 1991.
L. Pennati, G. Asnicar, *I monili del melodramma. Gocciole d'astri*, exhibition catalogue, Milan 1991.
M. Robbiani, *Gli orecchini, mito e seduzione*, Vicenza 1991.
1992
Var. Authors, *The Belle Epoque of French Jewellery 1850-1910*, London 1992.
Anni Venti. La nascita dell'abito moderno, exhibition catalogue, Florence 1992.
C. Cavey, *Gems and Jewels. Fact and Fable*, New Jersey 1992.
Fabergé e l'arte orafa alla corte degli Zar, exhibition catalogue, Genoa 1992.
L. Field, *The Jewels of Queen Elizabeth II. Her Personal Collection*, New York 1992.
J. Neré, *Ces bijoux qui font rêver*, Paris 1992.
Van Cleef & Arpels, exhibition catalogue, Paris 1992.
Ori e tesori del Friuli-Venezia Giulia, catalogue of the exhibition at Villa Manin, Passariano 1992.
Il tesoro Trieste, gioielli dalla Collezione Trieste e dalla Collezione Sartori-Piovene, exhibition catalogue, Padua 1992.
G. Vergani, *La Sala Bianca. Nascita della moda italiana*, exhibition catalogue, Florence-Milan 1992.

Extraordinary Jewels: An Adventure Beyond Style

Lodovica Rizzoli Eleuteri

Extraordinary jewels: what can we say about them? One thing stands out: it seems as if "something" essential and at the same time elusive, immediately recognizable even though very intimate—in a word, something necessary—links creations of different styles that are apparently remote from one another, allowing them all to be fitted into the category we are examining here, that of "extraordinary jewels." For there is, undoubtedly, something in common among such pieces of jewelry as the extremely elegant brooch-watch in pure deco style (plate 60), Vever's necklace with its highly restrained but sinuous lines (plate 6), the graceful ballerinas of Van Cleef & Arpels (plate 123), the bracelet of carved rubies that turns into a pendant (plate 74), the buckle (still in the art nouveau style) depicting two cornucopias (plate 8), and the forties necklace decorated with citrines.

So the immediate and persistent suspicion arises that it is something that goes beyond the market value of these objects, which in some cases is determined by the brazen laws of economics. And that goes beyond the obviously unifying characteristic from the aesthetic viewpoint, that of their extravagance. I have to admit that it is precisely the search for this something that has been the driving force behind the work I have carried out: research and reference, but above all selection and organization of the material according to criteria that emphasize the rigor of such a tempting project as the identification of "extraordinariness." Presenting the conclusions, and justifying them, is what I shall try to do in these pages.

Well: the something that unifies the extraordinary jewels that I have assembled here seems to consist in a response. More and better than others, but above all (unlike others) always and in every case, they provide a response—direct and incontrovertible, immediate and emblematic—to the demands that society has made from time to time from artistic jewelry. Shouted demands. Whispered demands. Unexpressed, and sometimes even strongly denied demands, since they were rooted in the collective unconscious. Demands to be interpreted and represented, to be sharpened or even outstripped. The figurative and extreme response to these demands, that is the *raison d'être* of these extraordinary jewels, and at the same time what they share in common—above and beyond all the differences—on a plane that therefore turns out (and this does not appear to be a paradox) to be one of absolute functionality.

The demands to which they have supplied a response have been highly disparate, over the course of this iron century that is now drawing to a close: to reformulate them here means looking back over the whole of the century from a clearly delimited perspective, the one offered by the most precious of the minor arts, by the recent history of taste, and setting out to look for the echoes stirred in it by some of the significant events in history on a larger scale. In fact it has been the privilege of these extraordinary jewels to reflect such events with limpid clarity.

Right at the beginning, then, arises the crucial problem of the relationship between artistic and industrial production, the great question raised, for example, by Paul Valéry in his *Pièces sur l'art*. Valéry wrote: "In all the arts there is a physical part that can no longer be viewed and treated in the same way as before, and that can no longer be separated from the effects of modern knowledge and power. Material, space, and time are no longer, for some twenty years now, what they had always been in the past. It is only to be expected that changes on such a scale should transform the whole of artistic technique, and in this way affect creativity

Van Cleef & Arpels, Necklace in polished yellow gold decorated with citrines, circa 1935. Private Collection.

itself, to the point perhaps of bringing about a marvelous modification of the very notion of art."

At the beginning, however, that "marvelous modification" tended to arouse fear in many artistic circles: in particular the fear of losing one's own identity, of being crushed by the frustrating repetitiveness of industrial processes. The world turned on its hinges, and art, a sensitive seismograph, perceived the enormous changes under way in the economy and society. The whole of art. But in the sphere of the minor arts, there was perhaps no more explicit response than the one provided by the extraordinary jewelry of the art nouveau style, whose categorical imperative could be expressed as follows: getting away from repetitiveness by giving free rein to the imagination, exorcising fear by taking refuge in the freedom of dreamlike phantasmagoria, and seeking the different and the exotic everywhere and by every means. The threatening menace of the industrial metropolis was spreading its tentacles? Then those tentacles were to be transformed into lianas, its gloomy shades challenged by the glowing colors of enamel, and flowers and birds in a thousand different forms were to took the place of alleys and streets, evoking an idealized rural world that at just that time was beginning to lose what had always been its central place in the familiar landscape of people's lives, giving way to urban settings. And if the distance created by fantasy turned out to be insufficient, there was always, in a world made smaller by the diffusion of the automobile and the airplane, the real distance of a far-off country like Japan, an inexhaustible source of inspiration.

Yet it is precisely in the congruity, in the extreme exactness of the response provided by these extraordinary jewels to the demands and requirements of a world in search of an impossible escape from industrialization and urbanization, that we must look for the reasons and the inner necessities for their replacement by another style. The more a response is targeted, the less flexible it can be, the less it can serve for every occasion. And the escape into fantasy and dream—the enchantment of the strange so ably interpreted by the extraordinary jewelry of art nouveau—could not provide an adequate response to the impact of two epoch-making, and closely connected, events that burst into history with the second decade of the twentieth century: I am thinking of the horror of the First World War, and the consequent emergence on the scene of mass society, to a great extent the child of the war economy and of the mobilization of populations. If industrialization had been a fairly slow process of innovation, painfully received in certain artistic circles and requiring sometimes difficult adjustments, the shock of the war and its consequences meant that it was no longer possible to resort to escapes into fantasy, lest this resulted in an incapacity to respond to the demands of an uneasy society and in a loss of touch with reality. But it has already been pointed out that the capacity to make a suitable response was the *raison d'être* of these extraordinary jewels: that in fact their stylistic language, that is to say their very essence, underwent a radical change in the twenties, beginning to speak in the terse and highly controlled accents of art deco. A style that should not, therefore, be seen, as has sometimes been claimed, as a pure and simple reaction to the soft and insinuating lines of art nouveau, as if there were an imaginary pendulum that produced oscillations first in one direction and then in its opposite, in a never-ending series. A view of stylistic questions, this, that tends to isolate them from the context in which they live, and that forces them into a barren determinism that could theoretically be fixed *a priori* once and for all. No: the reality that lies behind such pieces of jewelry as a miraculously elegant brooch of mother-of-pearl and brilliants, or a bracelet in which the refinement of the technique of execution is placed wholly at the service of an exceptional precision of form (plate 71), is far more rich and complex, and the demands to which it furnishes a response are far more important and deep-rooted than the ones proposed by a simple history of styles. It is only from an intense "auscultation" of life and its exigencies—and from the inescapable propensity to sublimate them in art—that can arise the rigor and coherence of a bracelet by Templier (plate 55); the precision with which Cartier develops its style in one of its brooches (plate 26); or the grace which characterizes a bracelet by Georges Fouquet, with its surprising interweaving of linear style and sense of color (plate 59).

I would like to dwell a moment longer on the multitude of implications inherent in the response provided by the extraordinary jewelry of the deco style to the changing demands of society, for it allows us to grasp the complexity and the profundity of the levels on which

Van Cleef & Arpels, Brooch in platinum, brilliant-cut, baguette, *and* navette *diamonds, decorated with emerald drops, circa 1928. It was made for the Princess of Hohenlohe. Van Cleef & Arpels Collection.*

Van Cleef & Arpels, "Egyptian revival" brooch in platinum, decorated with emeralds, rubies, sapphires, and onyxes, circa 1924. Van Cleef & Arpels Collection.

Seaman Schepps, Brooch in the form of a rooster, with rubies, emeralds, sapphires, and diamonds, circa 1960. Private Collection.

such responses take place, and at the same time appears to be capable of offering examples of general validity that may be extended to other creations of this type, although belonging to different styles.

It could be important to note, for example, how the jewelry of the twenties expresses, summarizes, and magnifies, drawing it forcefully to the attention, that genuine revolution in perspective that had overtaken the world of art as a whole after the First World War. In the last analysis, this revolution consisted in no longer taking the viewpoint of the artist and goldsmith, of the creator of extraordinary jewels, ill at ease in the face of the advance of industrial processes of production, and who reacted to them by introducing an excess of fantasy into his work and relying on technical skills that could not be matched by machines and mass production (as happened with art nouveau jewelry). Rather, it meant adopting the viewpoint of the public, indicating a direction in which it was necessary for the artistic product—and I do not use the word "product" lightly—to be in harmony with the people it was made for and with the spirit of the times. No longer rejection and flight, in short, but necessary confrontation. Assuming that artistic creativity is in fact determined by the general conditions of an age and by the customs prevalent in it, there ought to be a necessary link and a constant correspondence between the facts of real life and the "fictions" that art produces under the influence of those facts. For it is difficult to resist the pressures of the taste of the public, which "tolerates" only those objects that are in conformity with it. And so the principle to which the designers of jewelry adhered with indisputable if hazardous ingeniousness was that of the search for a correspondence between product and public: a search that was anything but fortuitous, and based on a relationship that was also a law of the market. Their creativity was also, at bottom, the fruit of calculation, of an intelligence whose inventions anticipated and went along with the hidden anxieties and passions of a society in precarious equilibrium, purifying them, refining them, and turning them into essential forms. Only in this way can we explain the capacity of these extraordinary jewels to express the most complex phenomena with a force, a lucidity, and an exceptional stylistic precision, bringing to light their concealed relationships and breaking them down into their elements to assemble new forms, as well as revealing the analogies that link one to the other in their representations. And so we have pieces of jewelry that are, at one and the same time, perfect "products" and creations which seem on the other hand to be the result of unconstrained inspiration, such as Van Cleef's brooch (plate 37), Mauboussin's bracelet (plate 48), or Janesich's sautoir (plate 62). Naturally, alongside these pure realizations, there were also those that interpreted—and it could not have been otherwise, in view of what has been said—the wishful thinking that the modern masses nursed in their hearts: examples of this are a Boucheron brooch in rock crystal with a carved piece of jade (plate 47), or two ethereal necklaces of brilliants that marry great elegance and extreme wearability (plates 77 and 78). Common to both kinds, however, remains the tendency to give a new, more abstractly symbolic dimension to the various "morphisms" of art nouveau. This sometimes resulted in forms that were terse to the point of coldness, as is also confirmed by the influences to which some extraordinary pieces of deco jewelry owe a more open debt, and that can be identified in contemporary movements in the figurative arts (especially Abstractionism and Cubism), and in archeology, in particular that of Egypt, through the influence of its geometric patterns. It would be difficult to find a better example, from this last point of view, than one of Van Cleef & Arpels's "Egyptian revival" brooches.

The radical change that took place in the world of art between art nouveau and art deco, referred to above, and which is particularly clearly reflected in these extraordinary jewels, is something that has survived, in essence, to the present day. This is implicitly acknowledged by studies of the subject that speak of the contrast between art nouveau and deco, while underlining the continuity between deco and the subsequent style, which is commonly referred to as retro. And within these limits the scheme can work, even though it leaves in abeyance and without explanation the reason why this transition should have taken place in a different way, in terms of an evolution rather than of a radical opposition. Nor could it be otherwise: such questions are destined to remain unanswered as long as we remain within the framework of a history of styles. And yet our curiosity impels us to go in search of one, given the distance that separates an extraordinary piece of deco jewelry from its retro counterpart with regard to the materials used, the techniques adopted, and the forms: in a word the very essence of the object. Evidently, contiguity does not mean similarity in results.

So to gain a deeper understanding of this process of transmutation of one style into the other, it will again be necessary to move away from a merely stylistic perspective, and approach the problem in the terms with which we are now familiar. In other words we must ask ourselves what new demand emerging from society the extraordinary retro jewelry was responding to—as usual in an emblematic and exemplary manner. The answer is so disconcertingly obvious that it provokes a degree of

Seaman Schepps, Brooches in the form of fish, circa 1960. *Above, "Mississippi" fish with diamonds, pearls, carved sapphires,* cabochon rubies, emeralds, and enamel. *Below, Fish with rubies, head and tail of diamonds, and a cabochon ruby for the eye. Private Collection.*

Van Cleef & Arpels, "Passe-partout" necklace, made up of five detachable brooches in the form of flowers decorated with yellow and blue sapphires and rubies, circa 1940. *Van Cleef & Arpels Collection.*

suspicion, as often happens with things that appear too easy: they were responding to the demands made by the affluent society that was becoming more and more firmly established after the Second World War, gradually approaching the levels of unbridled consumption characteristic of recent years (often condemned in words but which it is difficult to avoid in the facts). From this point of view, even a significant experience like that of the "poor" jewelry of the war years fits perfectly into the picture, and should be seen as the inevitable attempt, given the shortage of or restrictions on precious metals, to adapt to the same needs to which the ponderous jewelry of the fifties would also respond—though this time in a sumptuous manner, as far as the materials used are concerned. Notice, for example, what a web of (at first sight) unexpected relationships can be conjured up by a series of bracelets made in the forties, including one by Gubelin made entirely out of yellow gold (plate 108), when compared with a "flashy" necklace of yellow gold and brilliants (plate 158), platinum and brilliants (plate 159), or with a gaudy set in yellow gold and citrines by Mauboussin (plates 131-132).

Let us say straightaway that the suspicion referred to above turns out to be well-grounded. The concept of the affluent society appears to be too vague to suit our purposes: such a society makes many—too many—demands for consumption, and leaves open the reason why some of them met with that type of response, that is to say the response of the extraordinary retro jewelry. Everything becomes clearer if we place another concept alongside that of the affluent society: and look at their interaction: the concept of kitsch, a word that will have to be rescued once and for all from the semantic limbo (to use a euphemism) to which it seems to have been condemned. It is time, in other words, to make sufficiently clear the neutrality of the word and concept, recognizing that they provide a fundamental key to understanding some more recent artistic phenomena, including the extraordinary jewels of art deco. In this perspective the word kitsch, which once had no more than a weak and negative significance, can acquire positive connotations and a precise aesthetic weight of its own, if it is true, as has been said, that "aesthetics is a waste of construction."

What is this weight? If kitsch as it is commonly understood was based on the affluent society that created in order to produce (multiplicability) and produced in order to consume (perishability) without troubling to make any distinction between good and bad taste, and if kitsch could signify artistic garbage, the opposite of authentic, or rather a supermarket version of the authentic, i.e. distorted by something that brought the rare within the reach of all and was therefore "authentically false," then the challenge faced by the extraordinary jewelry of the fifties and sixties, its response to this situation, was that of inventing another kind of kitsch that turned its meaning completely on its head. As a consequence kitsch turned out to have unsuspected educational virtues (the assertion of good taste against, through, and therefore by means of bad taste). Instead of its normal dimension of the everyday, there was the creation of a refined and flexible art of living as a result of which the design of jewelry for mass production became essential. In short: extraordinary jewelry seemed to fully accept the reality of kitsch from the viewpoint of form, whereas in reality it was emptying it out from the inside and revealing itself to be an ironic interpretation, when not a fully conscious criticism, that, while accepting certain conventional models and exaggerating others, was actually deriding both. With this in mind, take a look at such jewelry as the brooch in the shape of a tank (a true testimony to an era, plate 94), or the Rolex bracelet-watch with a little dome (plate 109), or the mock-Hellenistic bracelet of solid gold (plate 172), or the necklace with medallions (plate 164). In comparison with these the two fish-shaped brooches by Seaman Schepps, or a black enamel bracelet by Van Cleef in the form of a dog (plate 186), or even the necklace decorated with five flowers that can be detached and used as brooches, almost look like creations of great sobriety.

A quite separate matter, parallel to the discussion we have been carrying out here, would be that of collecting and collectors, the destination by choice, I would almost say by necessity, of extraordinary jewelry. But that would really be another story.

To bring these comments to an end, it will suffice to mention that in the noble dimension of collection it is implicit, but obvious, that the emphasis is on the most typical characteristic of extraordinary jewels: the way that they are testimonies to their time, interpreting its spirit in the most suggestive way. In the past this prompted Julius von Schlosser to speak of "collections of art and of wonders" in connection with what always seems to have been their vocation.

The First Twenty Years
of the Century

1
Georges Fouquet, Bracelet composed of a ring of enameled gold in the shape of a serpent that curls three times around the wrist. Its head is made of opal and the eyes of rubies. Attached to the mouth, which rests on the palm of the hand, is a chain linking it to a ring worn on the finger, also made of opal, gold, and enamels, 1899. It was designed by Alphonse Mucha and made by Georges Fouquet for Sarah Bernhardt, who wore it when playing Cleopatra on stage. Private Collection. (Photo Christie's)

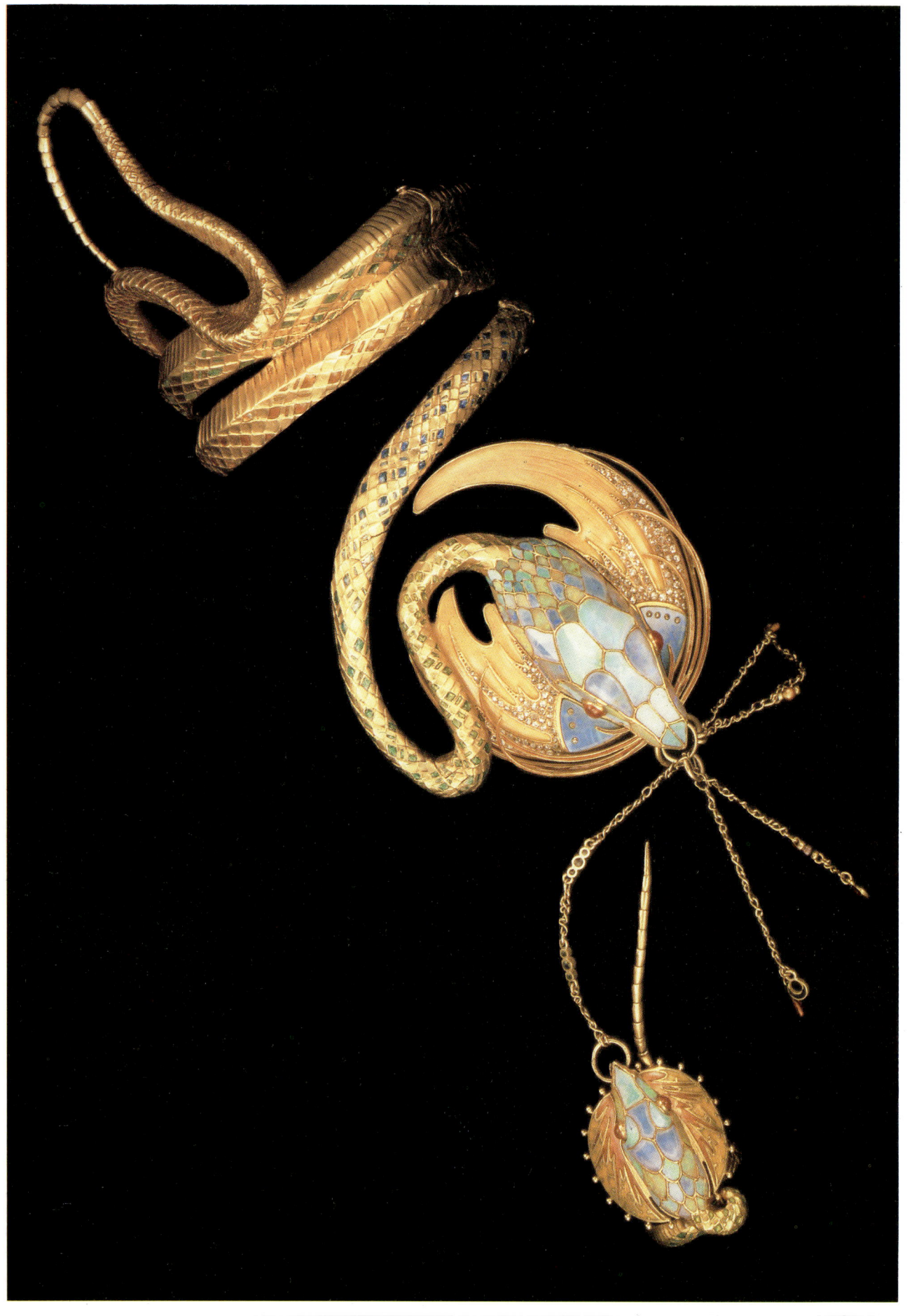

2
René Lalique, Plaque in the form of a bat whose wings are decorated with red and white enamel, and with inserts of opal glass. The body in the middle is made out of a baroque pearl, *circa* 1905. Private Collection. (Photo Christie's)

3
René Lalique, Bracelet with four medallions of carved glass depicting an allegory of the summer, alternating with convex plaquettes decorated with light green *pliqué-à-jour* enamels and motifs of sprigs of wheat in yellow gold, *circa* 1900. Private Collection. (Photo Sotheby's)

4
Georges Auger, Brooch in the form of a dragonfly made of silver and yellow gold and decorated with *pliqué-à-jour* enamel and diamonds (may be worn as an ornament for the hair), *circa* 1900. Private Collection. (Photo Christie's)

5
Lucien Gaillard, Comb with two dragonflies holding a citrine. The wings are made of carved horn with inserts of translucent enamels and rose-cut diamonds, 1903. Private Collection. (Photo Christie's)

6
Attributed to Henri Vever, necklace in a floral design with rose-cut diamonds, light green *pliqué-a-jour* enamel decorations in the shape of leaves, and five *cabochon* emeralds mounted like rose buds, *circa* 1900. Private Collection. (Photo Sotheby's)

7
Boucheron, Buckles of yellow gold: one represents two panthers biting a cornelian and standing on a piece of jade carved into the shape of a lion's head; the other, two fish holding a cornelian or citrine, 1900-8. Boucheron Collection.

8
Boucheron, Buckle of yellow gold composed of two cornucopias decorated with green enamel, 1903. Boucheron Collection.

9
Boucheron, Brooch of yellow gold and peridot, consisting of two griffin's heads facing one another and decorated with diamonds cut in the old-fashioned manner and a drop-shaped pendant of peridot, 1907. Boucheron Collection.

10
Boucheron, Bow-shaped brooch in darkened platinum and diamonds worked to create the effect of lace, 1908. Boucheron Collection.

11
Boucheron, Necklace of darkened steel decorated with natural pearls, diamonds, and zircons, 1900. Boucheron Collection.

12
Van Cleef & Arpels, Bracelet in platinum and brilliants, *circa* 1920. Private Collection.

13
Neiman Marcus, Necklace in yellow gold and green enamel, decorated with melon-shaped emeralds, *circa* 1900. Herriz Collection.

14
Mellerio dit Meller,
Necklace in yellow gold,
brilliants, and enamel,
1909. Mellerio dit Meller
Collection.

15
Mellerio dit Meller,
Brooch in white gold and
diamonds, last decade of
nineteeth century.
Mellerio dit Meller
Collection.

16
Cartier, Large bow-
shaped brooch in
platinum and brilliants
with four natural pearls,
circa 1910. Private
Collection.

17
Cartier, Bow-shaped
brooch in platinum and
brilliants with a yellow
natural pearl as pendant,
circa 1910. Private
Collection.

18
Tiffany, Brooch in platinum and brilliants with a large lozenge-shaped aquamarine in the middle, *circa* 1905. Private Collection.

19
Openwork bow in platinum, yellow gold, brilliant-cut diamonds, and square-cut emeralds, *circa* 1910. Private Collection.

20
Bracelets in platinum and diamonds decorated with openwork patterns, *circa* 1910. Private Collection. (Photo Christie's)

21
Bow-shaped brooch in platinum and diamonds decorated with floral patterns, *circa* 1910. Herriz Collection.

The Twenties and Thirties

22
Cartier, Bracelet-watch in platinum, carved emeralds, sapphires, rubies, and diamonds, *circa* 1925. Private Collection. (Photo Christie's)

23
Cartier, Pendent brooch-watch in coral, onyx, pearls, and diamonds, *circa* 1925. (Photo Sotheby's)

24
Cartier, Brooch in the form of a winged scarab carved out of smoky quartz, with *cabochon* emeralds, wings in antique blue faience decorated with emeralds and diamonds, 1924. Cartier Museum Collection.

25
Cartier, Bracelet with brilliant-cut and *baguette* diamonds, *circa* 1925. Private Collection.

26
Cartier, Brooch in platinum, brilliants, rock crystal, and black enamel, 1925. Cartier Museum Collection.

27
Cartier, Brooch in the form of a vase of flowers in platinum, *cabochon* emeralds, square-cut sapphires, rubies, and pearls, *circa* 1925. Private Collection.

28
Cartier, Bracelet in platinum, brilliants, and melon-shaped emeralds, *circa* 1925. Private Collection.

29
Cartier, Clip in platinum, brilliant-cut and *baguette* diamonds, and melon-shaped emeralds, *circa* 1930. Private Collection.

30
Cartier, Two clips in platinum and brilliant-cut and *baguette* diamonds, decorated with carved sapphires, rubies, and emeralds, *circa* 1930. Private Collection.

31
Cartier, Brooch in platinum and carved jade and lapis lazuli, *circa* 1925. Private Collection.

32
Cartier, Bracelet in platinum and *pavé* brilliants in the form of a row of tiny elephants, *circa* 1925. Private Collection.

33
Cartier, Necklace in platinum, diamonds, and thirty-nine pendent *cabochon* emeralds, 1938. It used to belong to the actress Merle Oberon. Zendrini Private Collection.

34
Cartier, Parure consisting of a necklace set with a frill of emerald berries, sapphire and emerald balls, sapphires and rubies, and thirteen *briolette* sapphires, and of carved emerald earrings with a motif of diamonds in the form of a calyx hanging from an emerald ball and a flower of diamonds.
It used to belong to Daisy Fellowes, who commissioned it from Cartier in 1936. Cartier Museum Collection.

35
Van Cleef & Arpels, Bracelet in the form of a garter made up of a flexible band of platinum decorated with brilliant-cut diamonds and with a stylized knot in the middle decorated with a cushion of sapphires and *baguette* diamonds, 1937. It used to belong to the Duchess of Windsor. Private Collection. (Photo Sotheby's)

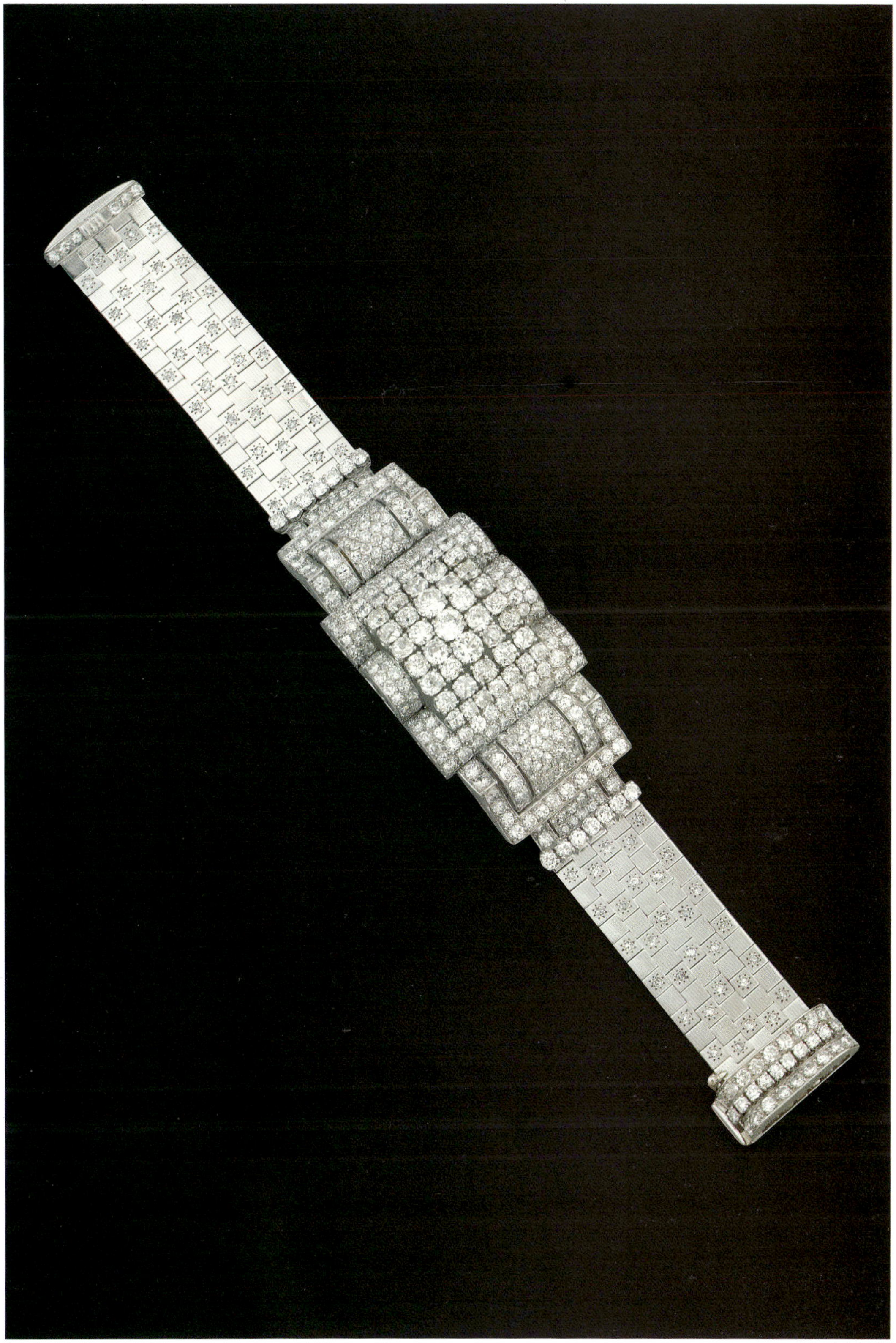

36
Van Cleef & Arpels, Bracelet with a "ludo" pattern in platinum and brilliants with a central section made of three bridging elements, 1939. Private Collection.

38
Van Cleef & Arpels,
Bracelet in platinum and
rubies, consisting of four
convex elements with
cushions of rubies,
interspersed with three
rows of brilliant-cut
diamonds. Designed
by René Dacaze and sold
in 1936 to King Edward
VII, who gave it to the
Duchess of Windsor.
Private Collection.
(Photo Sotheby's)

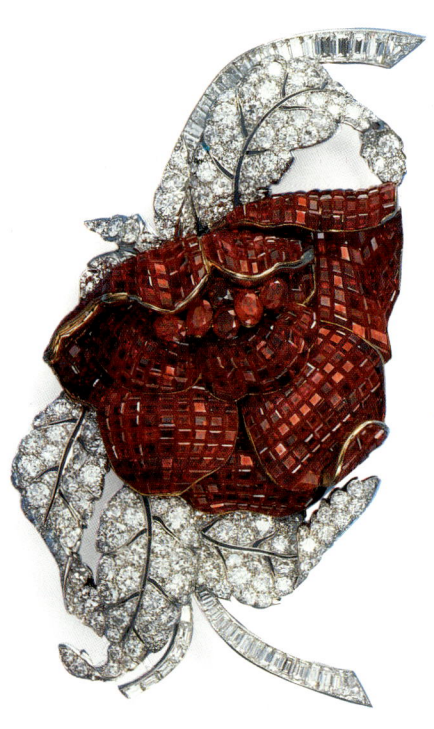

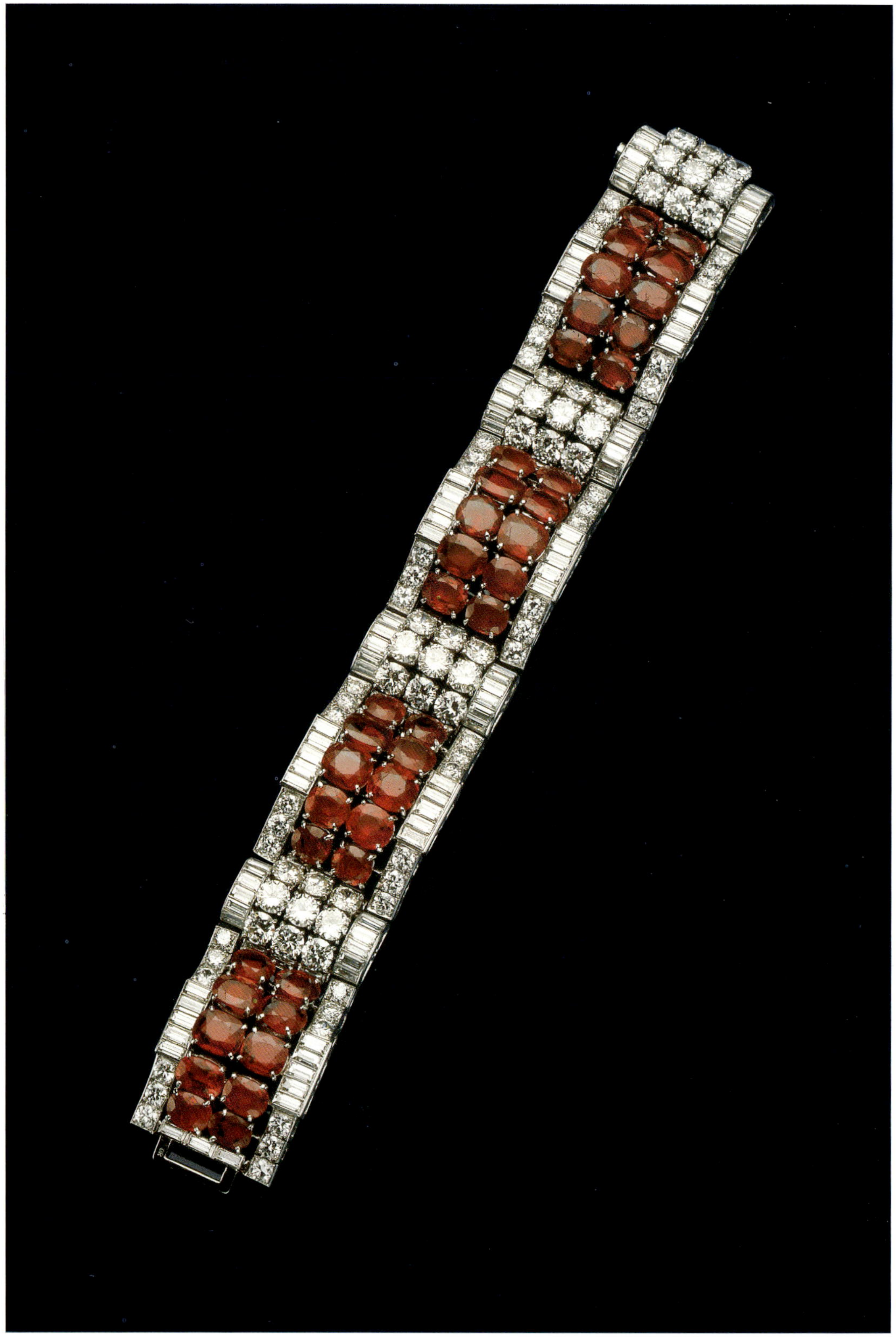

37
Van Cleef & Arpels,
Brooch in the form
of a rose with petals made
out of rubies set by the
technique of *sertes
mystérieux* and oval-cut
rubies. The leaves and
stem are in brilliant-cut
and *baguette* diamonds,
circa 1936. Private
Collection. (Photo
Christie's)

39
Van Cleef & Arpels,
Bracelet-watch in
platinum and brilliant-cut
and *baguette* diamonds,
1939. Private Collection.

40
Van Cleef & Arpels, Clips
in yellow gold, brilliants,
and imperial topazes set
by the technique of *sertes
mystérieux*, *circa* 1935.
Carlo Eleuteri Collection.

41
Van Cleef & Arpels,
"Egyptian revival" brooch
in platinum, brilliant-cut
diamonds, sapphires,
rubies, and emeralds; in
the middle, a yellow
sapphire, *circa* 1935.
Private Collection.
(Photo Sotheby's)

42
Van Cleef & Arpels, "Bird of Paradise" brooch in yellow gold; the feathers are decorated with *calibré* rubies, the beak is made of platinum and brilliants, and the eye is a *cabochon* ruby, 1942. Private Collection.

43
Van Cleef & Arpels, Necklace made up of two interlaced ribbon motifs, one decorated with diamonds cut *en baguette*, the other with cushions of Burmese rubies, 1936; a detachable motif of a cascade of rubies and diamonds in the middle was added in 1939. It used to belong to the Duchess of Windsor. Private Collection. (Photo Sotheby's)

44
Boucheron, Necklace in the form of a scarf, in platinum, rubies, emeralds, black onyx, and diamonds. It was shown at the Exposition des Arts Décoratifs in 1925. Private Collection. (Photo Sotheby's)

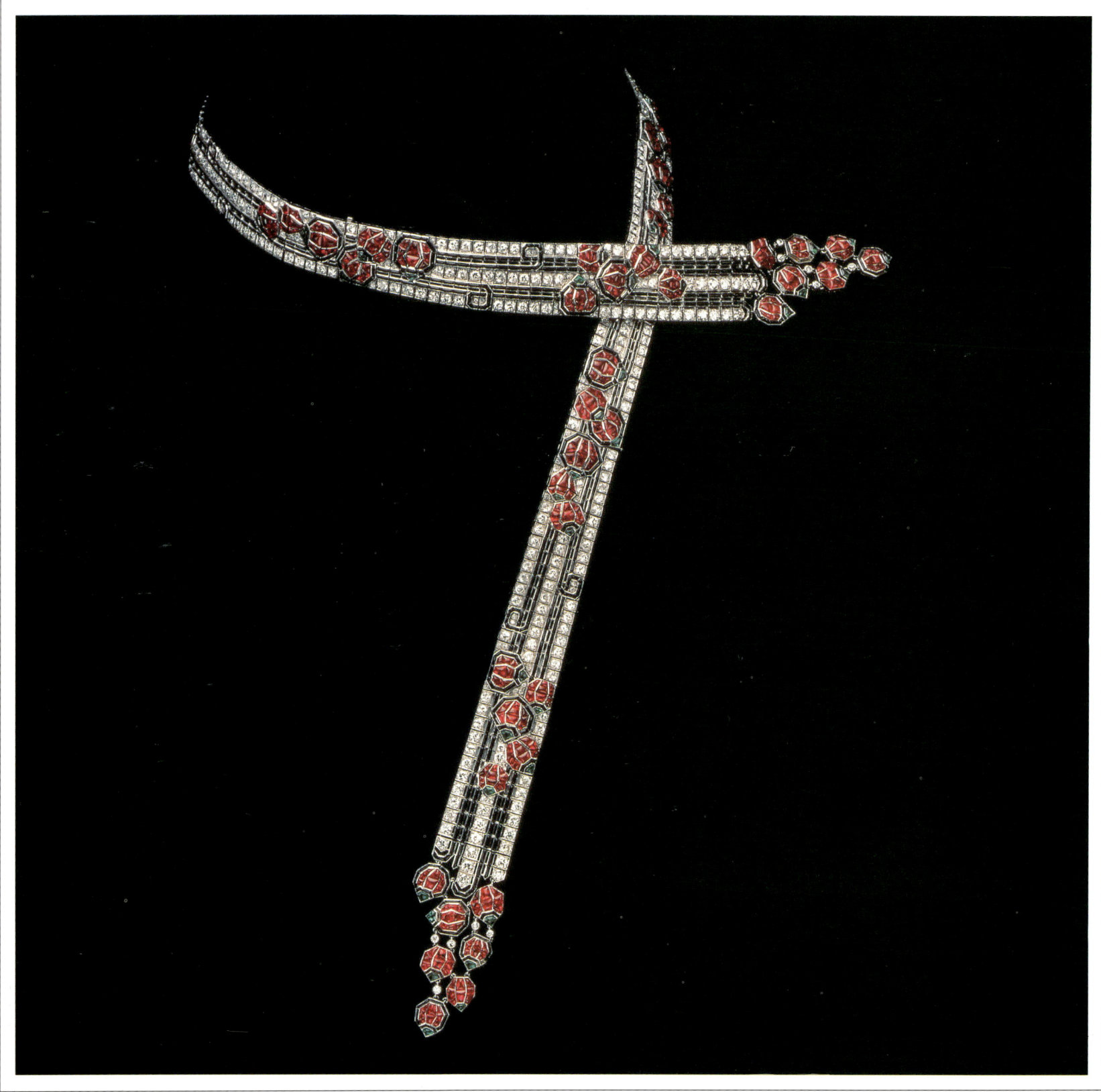

45
Boucheron, Pendent watch in platinum, lapis lazuli, and gray quartz decorated with diamonds, *circa* 1925. Boucheron Collection.

46
Boucheron, Watch with plaquette decorated with a checkered pattern of diamonds and red and black enamel; strap of black cloth, *circa* 1925. Boucheron Collection.

47
Boucheron, Brooch made up of a carved piece of jade set between two semicircles decorated with *pavé* diamonds, superimposed on two fans of carved rock crystal, 1934. Boucheron Collection.

48
Mauboussin, Bracelet in yellow gold decorated with plaquettes of coral, agate, and carved jade, *circa* 1925. Victor Arwas Collection.

49
Mauboussin, Brooch-pendent watch in platinum, brilliants, rock crystal, and carved jade, *circa* 1925. Victor Arwas Collection.

52
Mauboussin, Sautoir with pendent that can be used as a brooch, in platinum, diamonds, and carved emeralds, *circa* 1925. Private Collection. (Photo Sotheby's)

50
Mauboussin, Brooch-watch in platinum and brilliant-cut and *baguette* diamonds, decorated with carved rubies, emeralds, and sapphires, *circa* 1925. Mauboussin Collection.

51
Mauboussin, Brooch in rock crystal and diamonds, with carved emerald in the middle, 1928. Mauboussin Collection.

53
Mauboussin, Bracelet-watches in platinum and diamonds. Pendent watch in platinum and diamonds, 1925-30. Mauboussin Collection.

54
Mauboussin, Large rigid bracelet in platinum, brilliant-cut and *baguette* diamonds, and rubies, 1935-40. Private Collection.

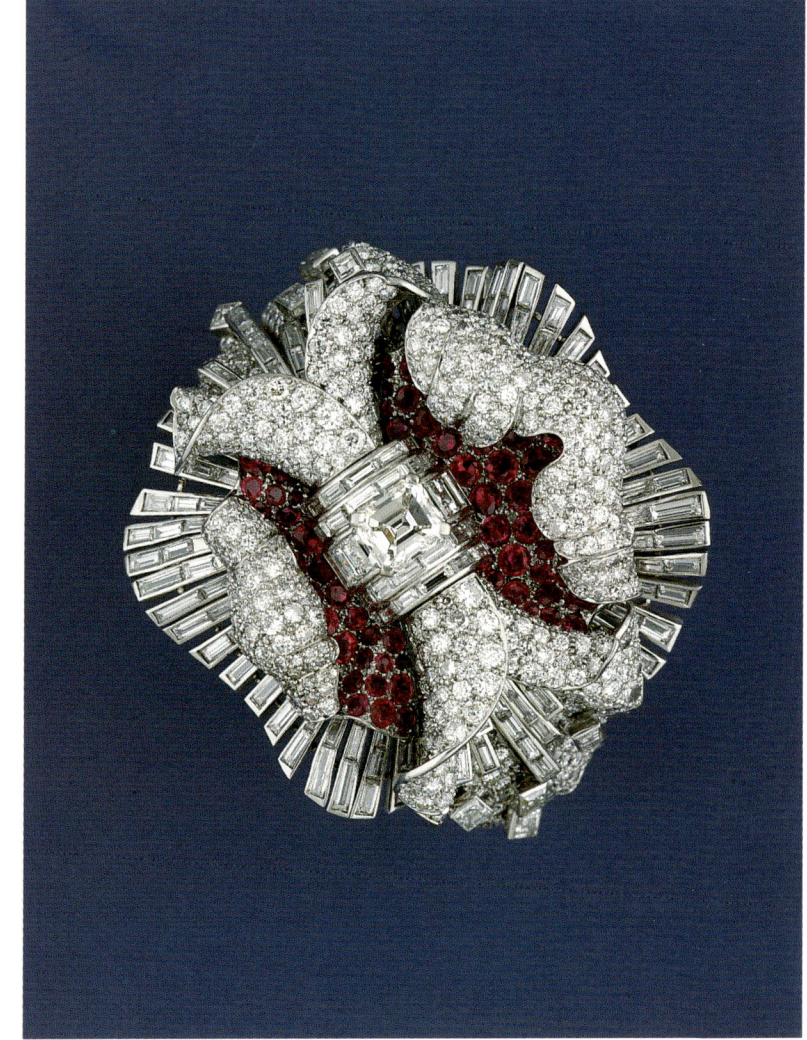

55
Raymond Templier, Bracelet in platinum, silver, onyx, and diamonds, made up of a large band of silver decorated in the middle with a geometric motif in white gold, onyx, and diamonds; the central part may be used as a brooch, *circa* 1925. Private Collection. (Photo Christie's)

56
Georges Fouquet, Brooch in platinum, coral, onyx, and diamonds, *circa* 1928. Private Collection.

57
Georges Fouquet, Brooch in platinum, diamonds, coral, and onyx, *circa* 1930. Private Collection.

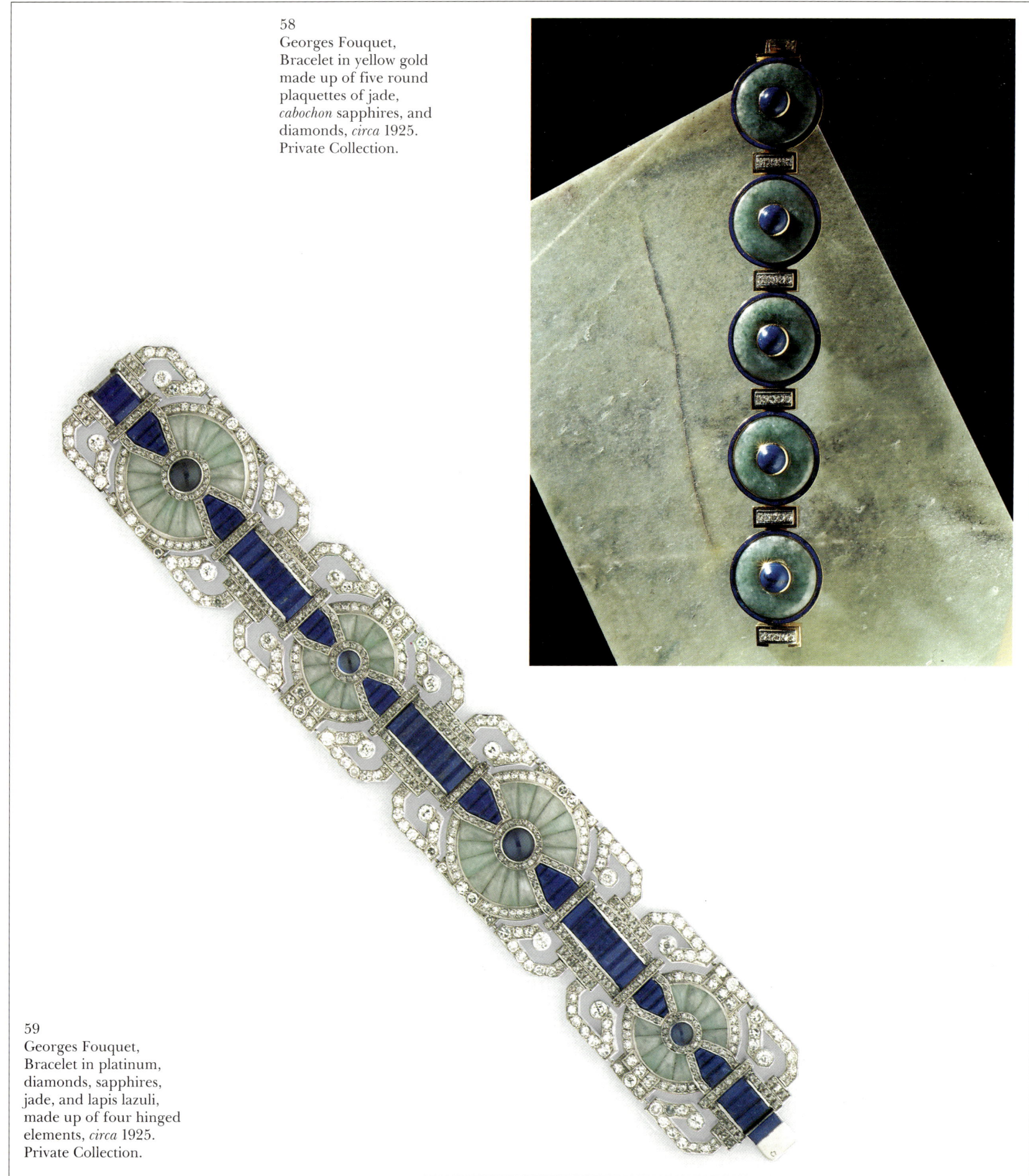

58
Georges Fouquet,
Bracelet in yellow gold
made up of five round
plaquettes of jade,
cabochon sapphires, and
diamonds, *circa* 1925.
Private Collection.

59
Georges Fouquet,
Bracelet in platinum,
diamonds, sapphires,
jade, and lapis lazuli,
made up of four hinged
elements, *circa* 1925.
Private Collection.

60
Ostertag, Brooch-watch in platinum and diamonds, decorated with emerald beads, *circa* 1925. Herriz Collection.

61
Lacloche, Bracelet in rock crystal carved in feline forms, black and green enamel, rose-cut diamonds, and carved rubies, *circa* 1925. Private Collection. (Photo Christie's)

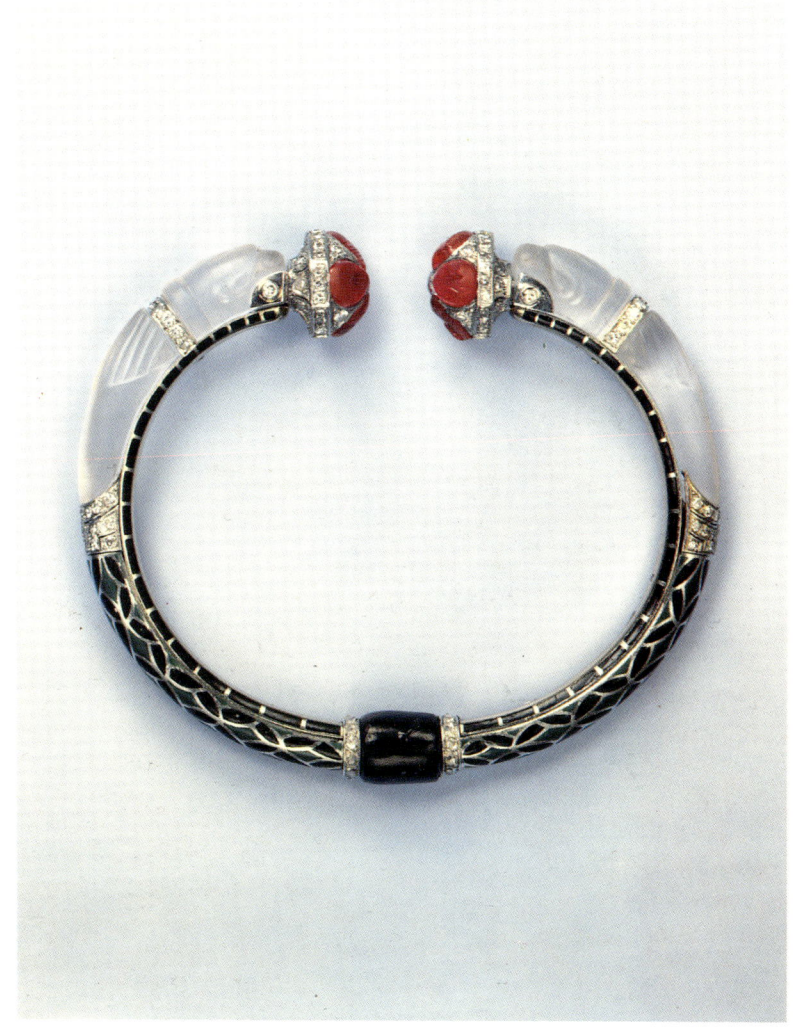

62
Janesich, Sautoir in platinum and diamonds with tassel-shaped pendant decorated with brilliant-cut and *baguette* diamonds, *circa* 1925. Private Collection. (Photo Christie's)

63
Buccellati, Bracelet in diamonds and brilliant- and rose-cut diamonds, *circa* 1930. Mario Buccellati Collection.

64
Buccellati, Geometrically patterned bracelet in yellow gold and rubies, 1935-40. Mario Buccellati Collection.

65
Mellerio dit Meller, Brooch in platinum, brilliant-cut and *baguette* diamonds; in the middle two natural pearls, 1938. Mellerio dit Meller Collection.

66
René Boivin, Wing-shaped brooch in yellow gold, diamonds, and sapphires, 1936. Private Collection. (Photo Sotheby's)

67
Suzanne Belperron, Bracelet and ring in smoky quartz decorated in the middle with a pattern of scales in diamonds and emeralds, *circa* 1935. Carlo Eleuteri Collection.

68
Pierre Sterlé, Brooch and earrings in platinum and brilliant-cut and *baguette* diamonds, *circa* 1930. Private Collection.

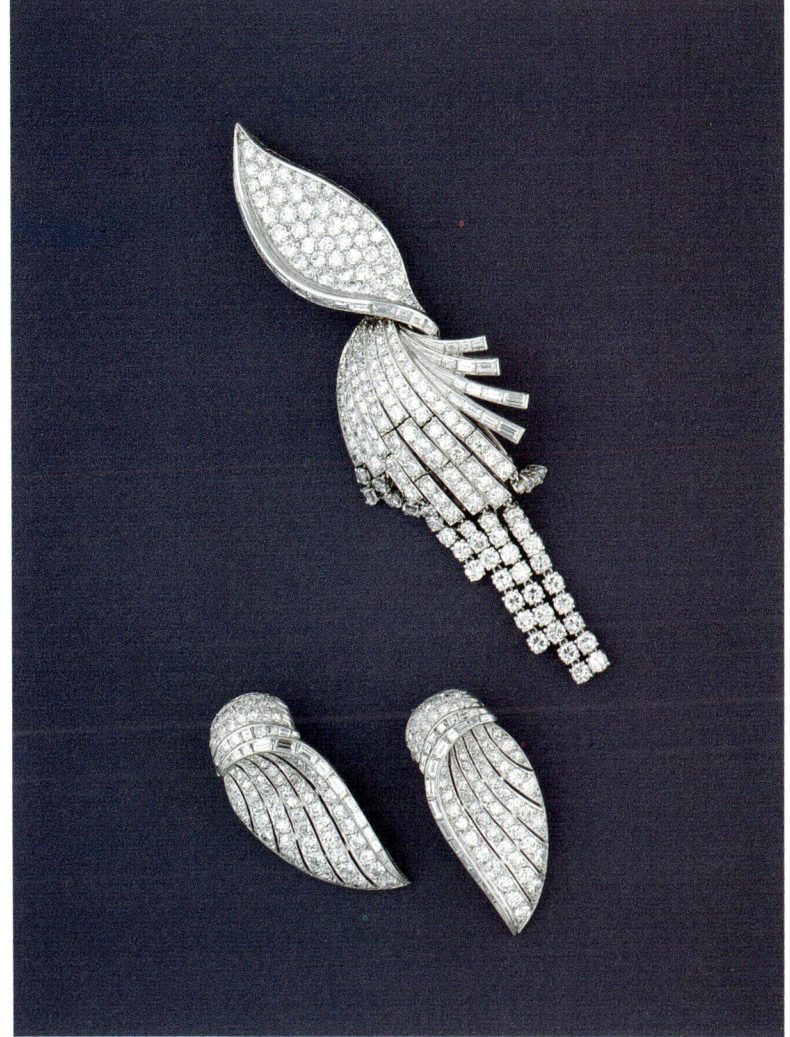

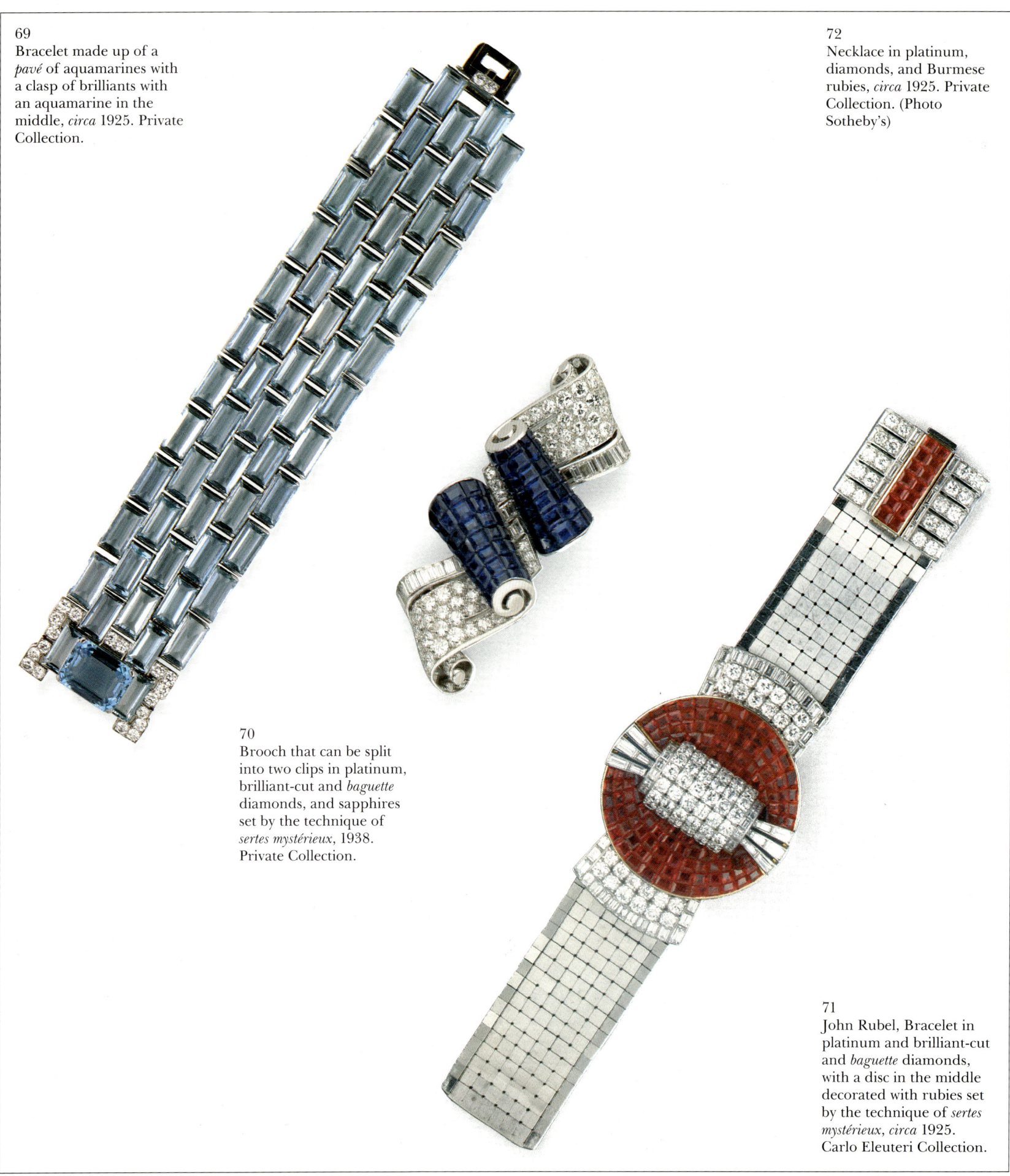

69
Bracelet made up of a *pavé* of aquamarines with a clasp of brilliants with an aquamarine in the middle, *circa* 1925. Private Collection.

70
Brooch that can be split into two clips in platinum, brilliant-cut and *baguette* diamonds, and sapphires set by the technique of *sertes mystérieux*, 1938. Private Collection.

72
Necklace in platinum, diamonds, and Burmese rubies, *circa* 1925. Private Collection. (Photo Sotheby's)

71
John Rubel, Bracelet in platinum and brilliant-cut and *baguette* diamonds, with a disc in the middle decorated with rubies set by the technique of *sertes mystérieux*, *circa* 1925. Carlo Eleuteri Collection.

73
Bracelet in platinum, brilliant-cut and *baguette* diamonds, and carved rubies, *circa* 1925. Private Collection.

74
Bracelet in platinum and brilliant-cut and *baguette* diamonds, with ruby balls and carved and *cabochon* rubies, *circa* 1925. Carlo Eleuteri Collection.

75
Bracelet in platinum and brilliant-cut and *baguette* diamonds, with three emeralds in the middle, *circa* 1930. Herriz Collection.

76
Turban ornament in openwork platinum, with brilliant-cut and *baguette* diamonds. In the middle a *cabochon* emerald carved with floral decorations. At the top a feather motif, from which hangs a drop-shaped emerald, *circa* 1930. It used to belong to the Maharaja of Baroda. Private Collection. (Photo Christie's)

77
Sautoir in platinum, brilliant-cut, *baguette*, and *navette* diamonds with a drop-shaped pendant that has a *briolette* diamond at its center, *circa* 1920. Herriz Collection.

78
Sautoir in platinum and brilliant-cut and *baguette* diamonds and pendant with a carved emerald, *circa* 1925. Private Collection.

80
Necklace in platinum, brilliants, and ruby beads, made up of a series of large carved emeralds, 1925-30. Private Collection.

79
Flower-shaped brooch in platinum with brilliants, square-cut emeralds, and a yellow sapphire in the middle, *circa* 1930. Private Collection.

81
Brooch depicting a bird decorated with black, green, and blue emeralds, set in a frame of a diamonds and black enamel, *circa* 1925. Private Collection.

82
"Egyptian-style" bracelet in platinum consisting of a band of *pavé* diamonds, decorated with Egyptian motifs formed out of sapphires, *cabochon* rubies and emeralds, and black onyx, *circa* 1925. Private Collection. (Photo Christie's)

83
Brooch in platinum and brilliant-cut and *baguette* diamonds, *circa* 1925. Private Collection.

84
Hinged bracelet in platinum, brilliants, and segments of glass paste decorated in the Japanese style, *circa* 1925. Private Collection.

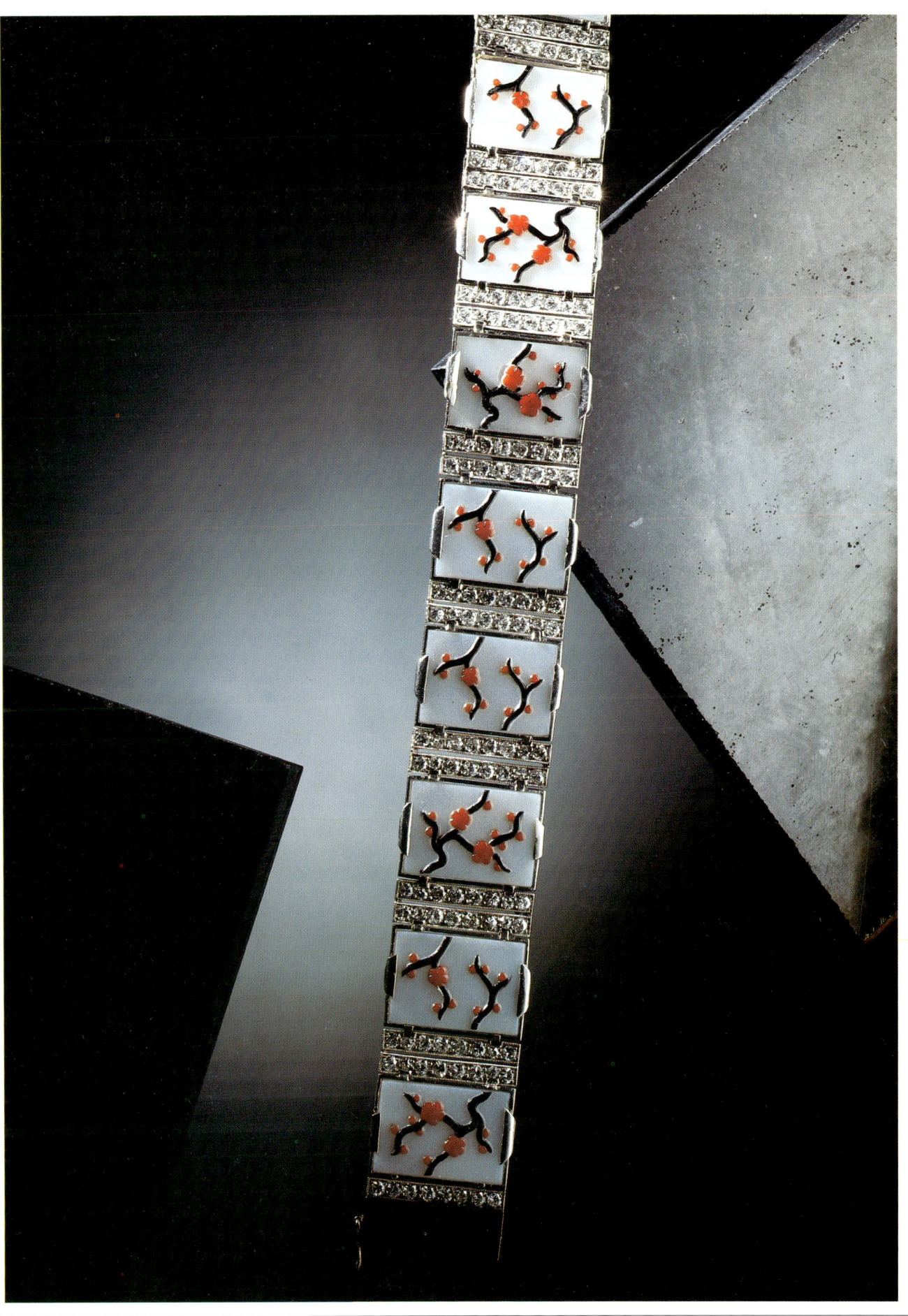

85
Bracelet in platinum and
brilliant-cut and *baguette*
diamonds, *circa* 1930.
Private Collection.

86
Ring in rock crystal
decorated with brilliants,
circa 1930. Private
Collection.

87
Butterfly-shaped earrings
in platinum and
diamonds, *circa* 1930.
Private Collection.

88
Earrings in platinum and diamonds cut *en baguette* and *en navette*, circa 1930. Private Collection.

89
Mauboussin, Bracelet in platinum and brilliant-cut and *baguette* diamonds, circa 1930. Private Collection.

90
Brooch that can be split into two clips in platinum and brilliant-cut and *baguette* diamonds, *circa* 1930. Private Collection.

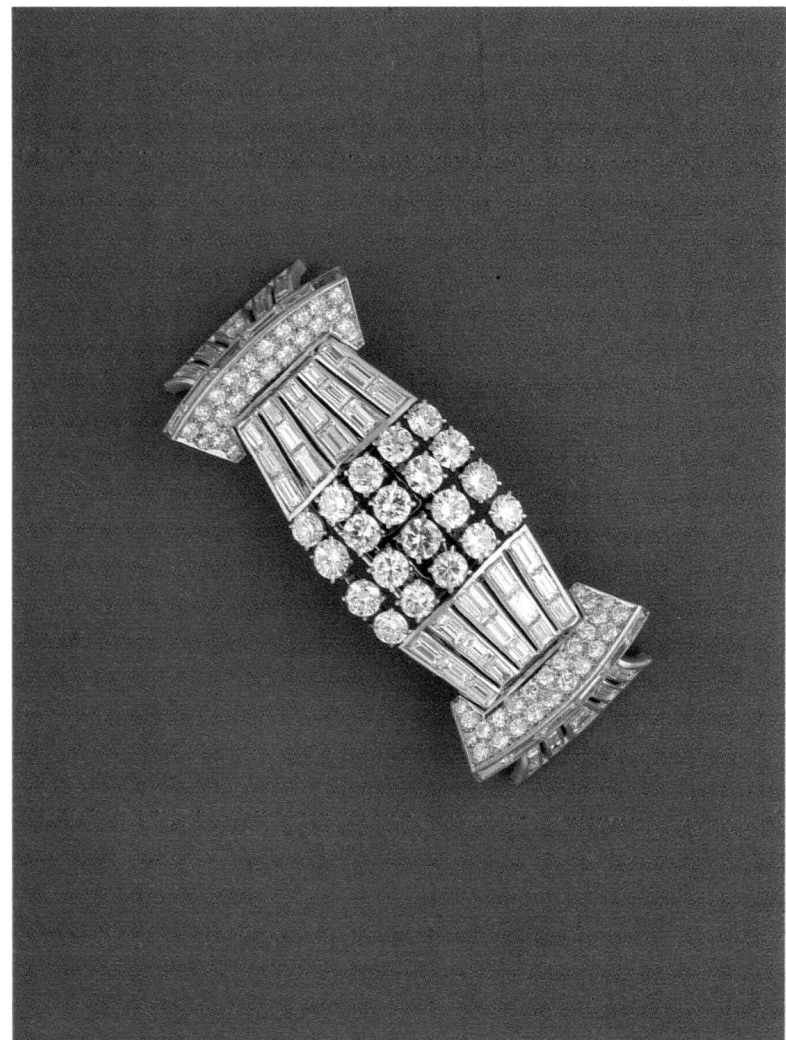

91
Bracelet in platinum and brilliant-cut and *baguette* diamonds, *circa* 1935. Private Collection.

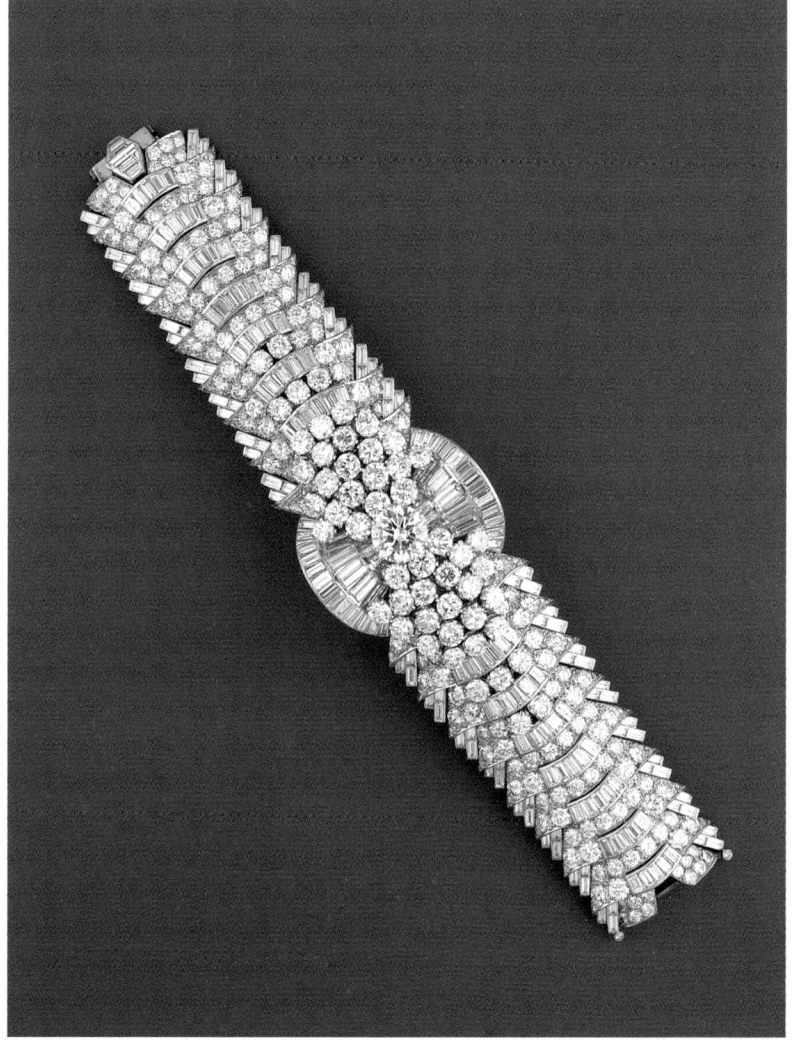

92
Bracelet-watch in yellow gold with clasp in platinum, brilliant-cut and *baguette* diamonds, and square-cut rubies, 1935-40. Private Collection.

93
Bracelet in yellow gold with central bridge-shaped motif decorated with a *pavé* of diamonds, 1935-40. Private Collection.

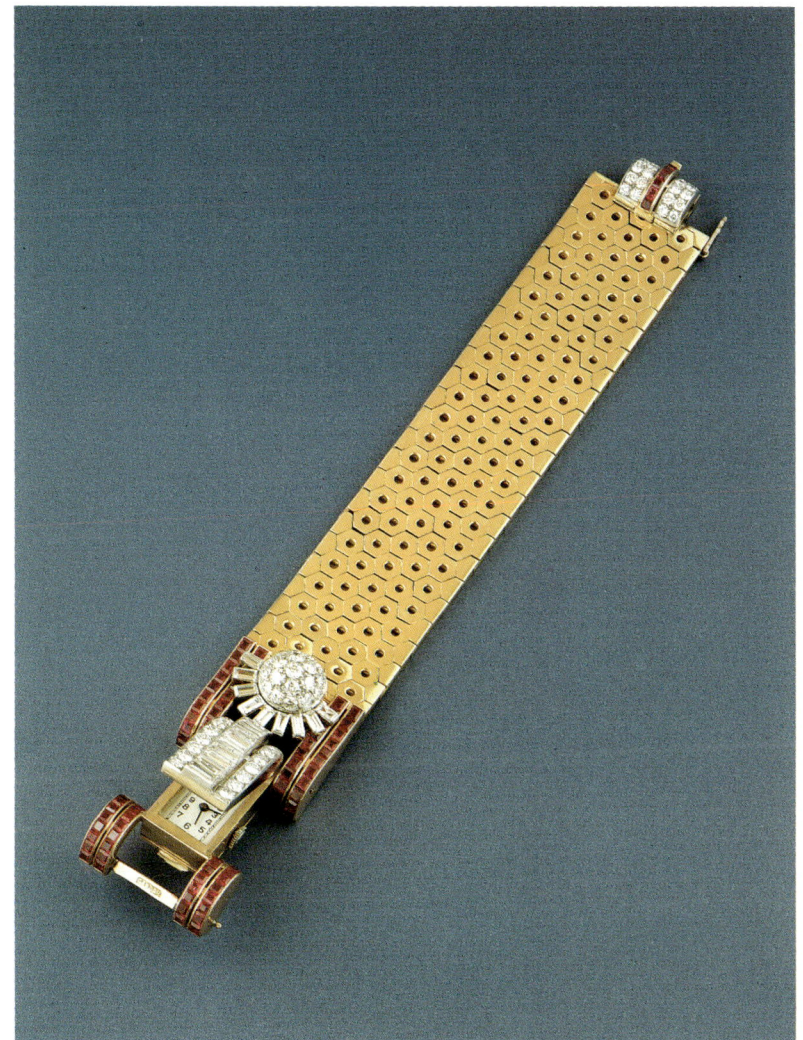

From the Forties
to the Sixties

94
Brooch in the form of
a tank in yellow gold with
ruby inserts, *circa* 1945.
Private Collection.

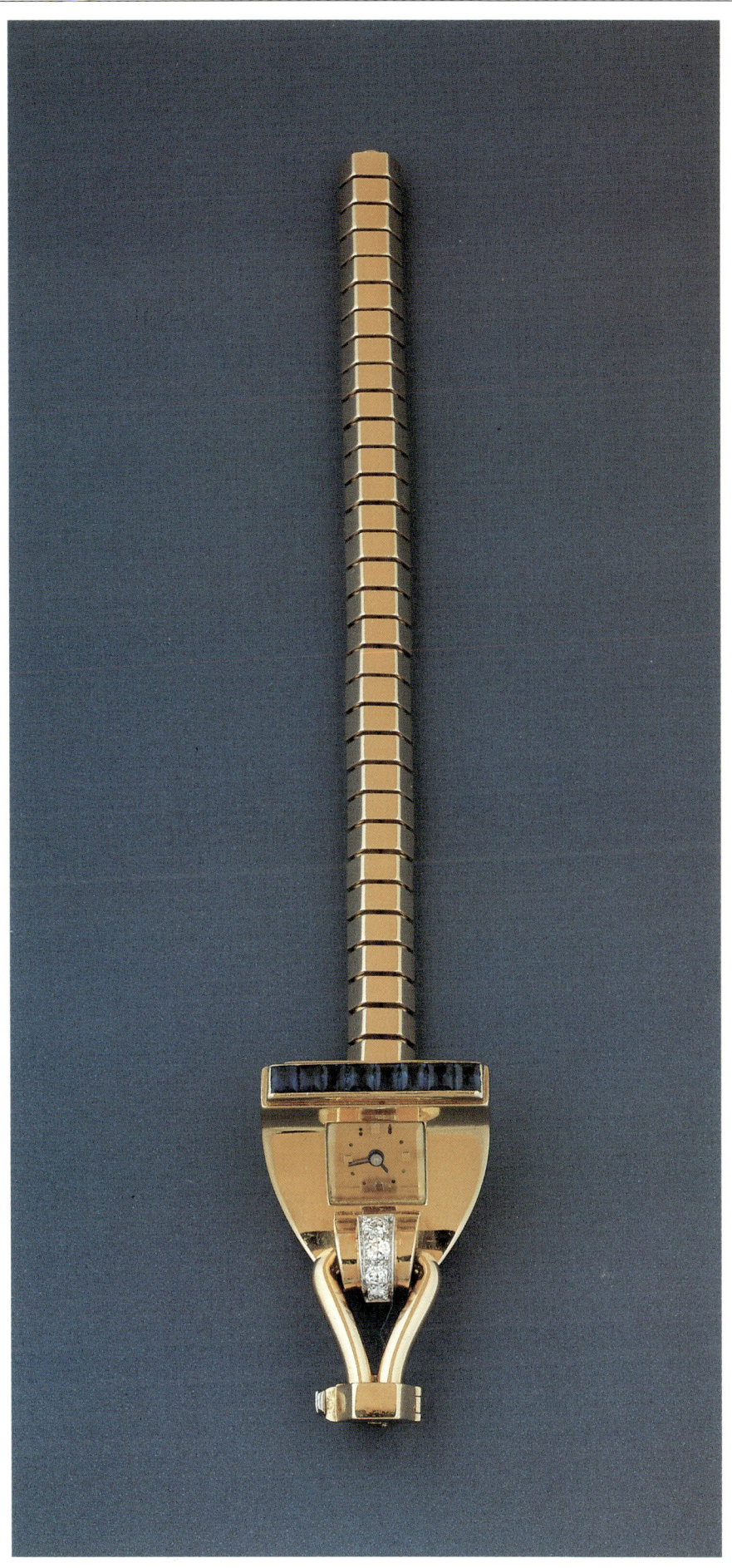

95
Boucheron, Bracelet-watch in yellow gold, square-cut sapphires, and diamonds, *circa* 1940. Boucheron Collection.

96
Boucheron, Bracelet in yellow gold and brilliant-cut diamonds with a twisted central element, *circa* 1940. Boucheron Collection.

97
Boucheron, Bracelet in yellow gold, brilliant-cut diamonds, and square-cut sapphires, *circa* 1940. Boucheron Collection.

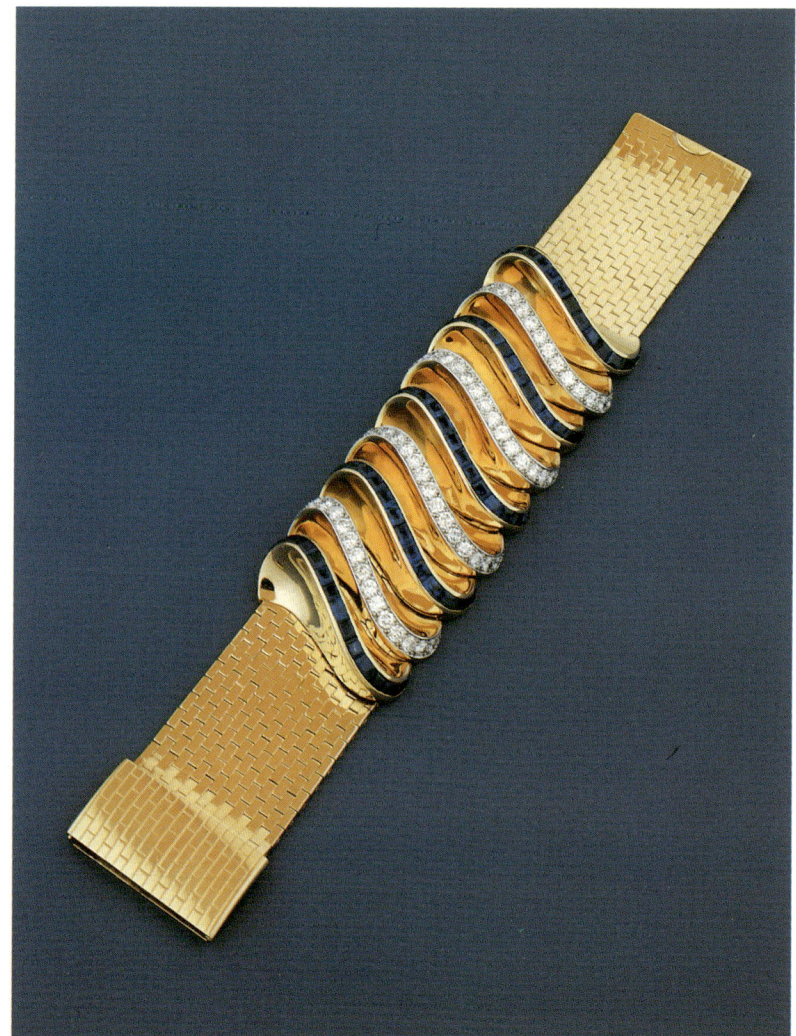

98
Boucheron, Bracelet in yellow gold and brilliants decorated with small leaf-shaped motifs, 1945-50. Boucheron Collection.

99
Boucheron, Floral brooch and earrings in yellow gold, diamonds, sapphires, and blue *pliqué-à-jour* enamel, 1940. Private Collection.

101
Boucheron, Necklace made up of two gold chains linked in the middle by a knot-shaped motif with a pendant in the form of an acorn; the stones are sapphires set in yellow gold and diamonds set in platinum, 1944. Boucheron Collection.

100
Boucheron, Brooch in yellow gold representing two flowers in citrines and diamonds, *circa* 1943. Boucheron Collection.

102
Boucheron, Bracelet in yellow gold decorated with undulating lines of brilliants and sapphires, *circa* 1950. Boucheron Collection.

103
Boucheron, Gold filigree brooches in the form of feathers decorated with rubies, sapphires, and brilliants, *circa* 1950. Boucheron Collection.

104
Mellerio dit Meller, Floral brooch in yellow gold, aquamarines, topazes, rubies, and sapphires; two flowers can be detached and used as earrings, 1940. Private Collection.

105
Lacloche, Bracelet in yellow gold and brilliants, *circa* 1940. Jina Laski and John Jesse Collection.

106
Bulgari, Necklace in yellow gold and brilliants made up of small shell-shaped motifs, 1940. Private Collection.

107
Bulgari, Two ball-shaped clips in yellow gold decorated with brilliant-cut diamonds. Gas-tube bracelet of yellow gold with balls at the ends decorated with brilliant-cut diamonds, *circa* 1940. Private Collection. (Photo Christie's)

108
Gubelin, Slightly curved bracelet made up of ten buckle-shaped motifs each containing five gold spheres and interspersed with rows of eight small gold spheres, *circa* 1945. Private Collection. (Photo Sotheby's)

109
Bracelet-watch in yellow gold with a small sky-blue hemisphere at the center decorated with diamond-studded stars (Rolex watch), *circa* 1940. Private Collection.

110
Gas-tube necklace in yellow gold with two leaves in the middle studded with brilliant-cut diamonds, *circa* 1945. Private Collection.

111
Cartier, Necklace made up of two strings of sapphire balls to which are attached nine floral motifs decreasing in size from the center, decorated with *cabochon* sapphires, brilliant-cut diamonds, and small arrowhead motifs in platinum and diamonds, *circa* 1940. It used to belong to the Duchess of Windsor. Private Collection. (Photo Sotheby's)

112
Cartier, Two bracelets in yellow gold, one decorated with sapphires, the other with rubies, set by the technique of *sertes mystérieux*, circa 1940. Private Collection. (Photo Christie's)

113
Cartier, Brooch in the form of a panther decorated with a *pavé* of diamonds and *calibré* sapphires, with pear-cut yellow diamonds for eyes. It rests on a large *cabochon* sapphire, 1948.
The brooch used to belong to the Duchess of Windsor. Cartier Museum Collection.

114
Cartier, Brooch in the form of a flamingo in its characteristic pose, in platinum decorated with *pavé* diamonds and *calibré* emeralds, rubies, and sapphires, *circa* 1940. It was designed and created by Jeanne Toussaint. The brooch used to belong to the Duchess of Windsor. Private Collection. (Photo Sotheby's)

115
Cartier, Parure consisting of bracelet, necklace, and ring in platinum, diamonds, and aquamarines cut in various ways, *circa* 1940. Private Collection. (Photo Christie's)

116
Cartier, Parure consisting of bracelet, brooch, and earrings in the form of tigers, in yellow diamonds and black onyx, 1955. It used to belong to Barbara Hutton. Private Collection. (Photo Sotheby's)

117
Cartier, Necklace in platinum and brilliant-cut and *baguette* diamonds, with a cascade motif of Burmese rubies in the middle, 1948. Carlo Eleuteri Collection.

118
Cartier, Bangles in diamonds and rock crystal, *circa* 1950. They used to belong to Gloria Swanson. Private Collection. (Photo Christie's)

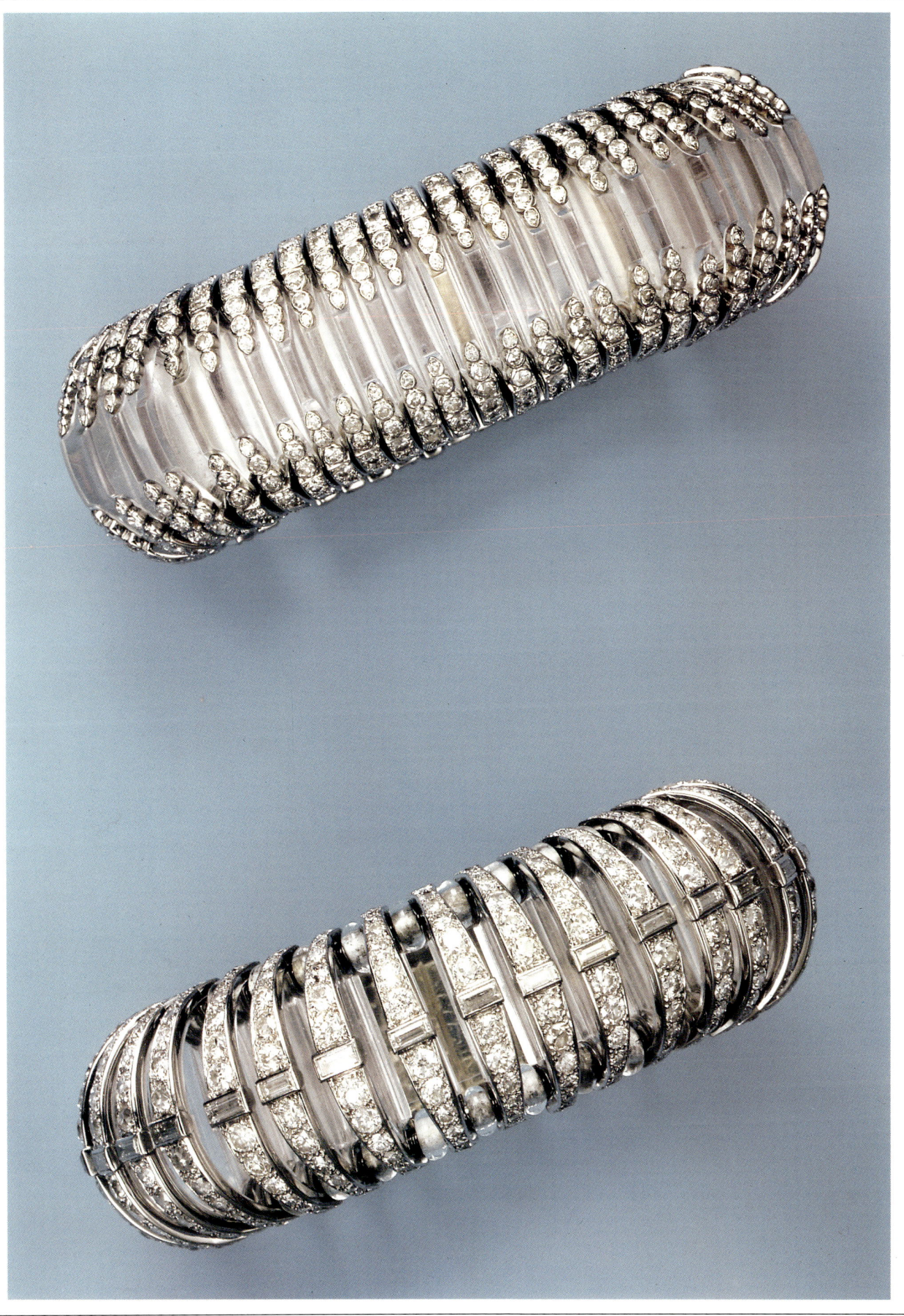

120
Cartier, Brooch in the form of a rose in coral and diamonds, *circa* 1960. Private Collection. (Photo Christie's)

119
Cartier, Bracelet in the form of a chimera in carved coral, brilliant-cut diamonds, and *cabochon* emeralds; each head is decorated with a pear-cut diamond, *circa* 1954. Private Collection. (Photo Christie's)

121
Cartier, Parure consisting of necklace, brooch, bracelet, and earrings formed out of small strawberry-shaped motifs in yellow gold decorated with brilliant-cut diamonds, rubies, and emeralds, *circa* 1960. Private Collection. (Photo Christie's)

122
Cartier, Brooch in the form of a bird in amethyst, emeralds, and brilliants, *circa* 1960. Private Collection.

123
Van Cleef & Arpels, Brooches in the form of ballerinas in platinum, with their heads formed out of pear- or rose-cut diamonds, outlined by rubies and emeralds; the costumes are decorated with rose-cut diamonds, rubies, and emeralds, 1944. Private Collection. (Photo Van Cleef & Arpels)

124
Van Cleef & Arpels, Semirigid bracelet in platinum, diamonds, and emeralds, 1947. Private Collection.

125
Van Cleef & Arpels and David Webb, Rigid bracelet-watch in platinum, diamonds, yellow sapphires, and emeralds. It is made up of a panther designed by David Webb and a watch designed by Van Cleef & Arpels, *circa* 1950. Private Collection.

126
Van Cleef & Arpels, Brooch in the form of a rose in coral, leaves in yellow gold decorated with sapphires and diamonds, 1960. Private Collection.

128
Traebert & Hoeffer and Mauboussin, Rigid bracelet in yellow gold, platinum, brilliants, and *cabochon* emeralds, *circa* 1940. It used to belong to Paulette Godard, who was given it by Charlie Chaplin to console her for having been rejected for the role of Scarlett in *Gone with the Wind*. Mauboussin Collection.

127
Mauboussin, Brooch in the form of a heart in yellow gold, white gold, *cabochon* rubies, and diamonds, 1940. N.P. Collection.

129
Mauboussin, Rigid bracelet in yellow gold, diamonds, and sapphires, *circa* 1940. Private Collection.

130
Mauboussin, Necklace in yellow gold with interlaced central motif decorated with rubies, sapphires, and emeralds, *circa* 1950. Mauboussin Collection.

131-132
Mauboussin, Parure consisting of knot-shaped brooch in yellow gold and square-cut citrines, bracelet and earrings in yellow gold and citrines, 1945-50. Private Collection.

133
Mauboussin, Brooch in yellow gold, brilliant-cut and *baguette* diamonds, and aquamarines cut in various ways, *circa* 1940. Private Collection.

134
Mauboussin, Bracelet and earrings in yellow gold decorated with multicolored *cabochon* stones (sapphires, rubies, emeralds); the central part of the bracelet turns into two clips, *circa* 1940. Private Collection.

135
Mauboussin, Floral clips in yellow gold and platinum, blue and yellow sapphires, rubies, and carved emeralds, *circa* 1950. Mauboussin Collection.

136
Mauboussin, Feather-shaped brooch in yellow gold decorated with carved emeralds, sapphires, and rubies, and brilliants, *circa* 1950. Mauboussin Collection.

137
Mauboussin, Brooch in the form of a butterfly decorated with carved emeralds and rubies; the wings are made of *pliqué-à-jour* enamel bordered with brilliant-cut diamonds and *calibré* sapphires. Four *cabochon* emeralds are set at the tips of the wings, *circa* 1950. Private Collection. (Photo Christie's)

138
Mauboussin, Chain in yellow gold and brilliants from which hangs a ram's head in carved rock crystal with eyes of emerald, *circa* 1960. Private Collection.

140
Mellerio dit Meller, Jabot necklace in yellow gold, citrines, and rubies, 1949. Mellerio dit Meller Collection.

139
Traebert & Hoeffer and Mauboussin (Reflection Collection), Brooch in yellow gold, diamonds, false topazes, and large *cabochon* emerald, *circa* 1953. Private Collection.

141
Neiman Marcus, Rigid bracelet in yellow gold, citrines, turquoise, rubies, and brilliants, *circa* 1950. Private Collection.

142
Black Starr & Frost, Brooch in the form of a butterfly in brilliants, carved Bakelite, and *cabochon* rubies and sapphires, *circa* 1930. N.P. Collection.

143
Fulco di Verdura, Brooch in the form of a scallop shell decorated with turquoise cut *en cabochon* and diamonds, set in yellow gold, *circa* 1940. Private Collection. (Photo Christie's)

144
Marchack, Brooch in the form of a mermaid in yellow gold, sapphires and brilliants; the head is made of rose quartz, *circa* 1960. Private Collection.

145
Petochi, Spring bracelet in platinum, brilliant-cut diamonds, and square-cut emeralds, *circa* 1950. Herriz Collection.

146
Serafini, Brooch in the form of a rooster in yellow gold, false topaz, amethysts, sapphires, rubies, diamonds, and green enamel, 1955-60. Private Collection.

147
Tiffany, Brooch in yellow gold and diamonds, with an oval citrine in the middle, *circa* 1950. Private Collection.

148-149
Tiffany, Brooches in yellow gold and colored enamel, representing Napoleon and Nelson, *circa* 1955. Private Collection.

150
Pierre Sterlé, Brooch in the form of a swallow in yellow gold, labradorite, and diamonds; another brooch in platinum and brilliant-cut and *baguette* diamonds, *circa* 1950. Private Collection. (Photo Christie's)

151
René Boivin, Two brooches in yellow gold in the form of starfish, one decorated with *cabochon* rubies and amethysts, the other with oval-cut emeralds on a base of small aquamarines, *circa* 1950. Private Collection. (Photo Sotheby's)

152
Chaumet, Trophy brooch with horse's head, helm, sword, and banners, in yellow gold, coral, mother of pearl, and diamonds cut *en navette* and *en baguette*, *circa* 1960. Private Collection.

153
Garrard, Necklace in yellow gold in the form of a snake whose head is formed by a drop-shaped fancy-brown brilliant, *circa* 1960. Private Collection.

154
Seaman Schepps, Clips in yellow gold, brilliants, and *cabochon* sapphires, emeralds, and rubies, *circa* 1960. Private Collection.

155
Seaman Schepps, Rigid bracelet in platinum, brilliant-cut and *baguette* diamonds, and rubies, decorated with large *cabochon* sapphires, *circa* 1960. Private Collection.

156
Frascarolo, Brooches representing two heads, one of a panther and the other of a leopard, in yellow gold, black enamel, and brilliants, *circa* 1960. Private Collection.

157
Gerard, Bracelet in yellow gold and brilliant-cut diamonds made up of a series of knots, *circa* 1960. Private Collection.

158
Gas-tube necklace in yellow gold decorated with brilliants, *circa* 1940.
Private Collection.

159
Necklace in brilliant-cut and *baguette* diamonds, *circa* 1940.
Private Collection.

160
Brooch in yellow gold, diamonds, and *cabochon* rubies, with an aquamarine in the middle, *circa* 1940. Private Collection.

161
Mauboussin, Brooch in platinum, diamonds and square-cut aquamarines, with a large aquamarine in the middle, *circa* 1940. Private Collection.

162
Brooch in the form of a daisy in yellow gold, platinum, and brilliant-cut and *baguette* diamonds. The central part rotates and is decorated with yellow sapphires and brilliants, *circa* 1940. Private Collection.

163
Brooch and earrings in yellow gold, platinum, square-cut sapphires, and diamonds, *circa* 1940. Private Collection.

164
Necklace in gold with souvenir medallions decorated with various precious stones, *circa* 1945. Private Collection.

165
Rigid bracelet in platinum decorated with a honeycomb pattern of aquamarines and a large central aquamarine, *circa* 1950. Private Collection.

166
Bracelet formed of a solid band of yellow gold and enamel decorated with applications in an art nouveau style with diamonds, sapphires, rubies, and aquamarines, *circa* 1950. Private Collection.

167
Bracelet in platinum, brilliant-cut diamonds, onyx, rock crystal, and a carved star sapphire, 1950. Claudio Zanettin Collection.

168
Clips in yellow gold and brilliants in the form of long leaves with inserts decorated with rubies, *circa* 1950. Private Collection.

169
Spray brooch in platinum, yellow gold, brilliants, and emeralds, *circa* 1950. Private Collection.

170
Brooch in the form of a flower in yellow gold, platinum, and brilliants. It can be removed from its support of yellow gold and used as a completely white brooch, *circa* 1950. Private Collection.

171
Bracelet in yellow gold, sodalite, diamonds, and citrine terminating in an eagle's head, *circa* 1960. Private Collection.

172
Bracelet in yellow gold representing a lion struggling with a snake, *circa* 1960. Private Collection.

173
Bracelet in yellow gold representing two bulls facing one another, *circa* 1960. Private Collection.

174
Brooch in yellow gold, citrines, and rubies, *circa* 1960.
Private Collection.

175
Brooch in the form of a frog in yellow gold, green enamel, rubies, and diamonds; it holds a piece of pink coral, *circa* 1960.
Private Collection.

176
Brooch in the form of an elephant in yellow gold, rubies, diamonds, sapphires, and carved emeralds, *circa* 1960.
Private Collection.

177
Brooch in the form of a turtle in malachite studded with brilliants, surrounded by carved pieces of coral, *circa* 1960.
Private Collection.

178
Pierre Sterlé, Fringed necklace in yellow gold and brilliants, *circa* 1950.
Private Collection.

180
David Webb, Rigid bracelet in coral, yellow gold, black enamel, and brilliants, in the form of two dragon's heads, *circa* 1960. Private Collection.

179
David Webb, Brooch in the form of a bull in yellow gold, diamonds, and red enamel, with emeralds for eyes, *circa* 1960. Private Collection.

181
David Webb, Brooch in coral, brilliant-cut diamonds, and *cabochon* sapphires and emerald, 1947. Claudio Zanettin Collection.

182
David Webb, Bracelet in the form of an elephant in yellow gold and jade, with rubies for eyes, *circa* 1960. Private Collection.

183
David Webb, Bracelet in yellow gold and rough diamonds, *circa* 1960. Private Collection.

184
David Webb, Bracelet in yellow gold, black enamel, and diamonds, *circa* 1960. Private Collection.

185
David Webb, Rigid bracelet in yellow gold with geometric inserts of diamonds and black enamel. In the middle a plaque of carved jade, *circa* 1960. Private Collection.

186
Van Cleef & Arpels, Bracelet in the form of a dog in yellow gold, black enamel, pink coral, diamonds, and emeralds, *circa* 1960.
Private Collection.

187
David Webb, Bracelet in the form of a zebra in yellow gold and black enamel, decorated with brilliants and emeralds for the eyes, *circa* 1960.
Private Collection.

188
David Webb, Bracelet in the form of a dolphin in yellow gold, carved coral, brilliants, sapphires, a *cabochon* ruby, and emeralds for eyes, *circa* 1960. Private Collection.

189
David Webb, Bracelet in the form of chimera's heads in polished yellow gold, diamonds, and emeralds, *circa* 1960. Private Collection.

190
David Webb, Pendant for necklace in the form of a dragon carved out of jade, with carved rubies and emeralds, *circa* 1960. Private Collection.

191
David Webb, Chain necklace in yellow gold and coral with pendant that can be used as a brooch, *circa* 1960. Private Collection.

193
David Webb, Necklace in yellow gold, diamonds, and pink coral, with pendant that can be used as a brooch, 1960. Private Collection.

194
David Webb, Necklace in yellow gold with pendant of Oriental inspiration, decorated with blue enamel, rose-cut diamonds, and rubies, *circa* 1955. Carlo Eleuteri Collection.

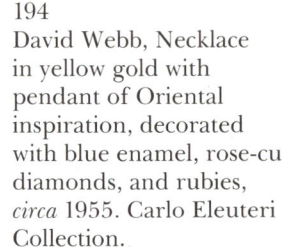

192
David Webb, Two rings in yellow gold, one decorated with diamonds, the other with white enamel, *circa* 1960. Private Collection.

147

Index of Jewelers

(The italics indicate the page numbers where captions appear.)

Arpels, Charles 18
Arpels, Claude 17
Arpels, Julien 18
Arpels, Louis 23
Aucoc 11
Aucoc, Louis 12, 14
Auger, Georges *40*

Backes, Georg Carl 7
Belperron, Suzanne *75*
Blake Starr & Frost *120*
Boivin, René *74, 124*
Bongard, Nicolas 22
Boucher, Marcel 20
Boucheron 11, 18, 24, 26, 28n, 34, *41, 42, 43, 44, 64, 65, 91, 92, 94, 95*
Boucheron, Frédéric 13
Braque, Georges *24, 27*
Buccellati *73*
Bulgari 24, *97, 98*

Capello 11
Cartier 8, 10, 11, 12, 15, 17, 18, *18*, 20, 21, 22, *22*, 25, 26, 28, 32, 34, 47, *52, 53, 54, 55, 56, 57, 58, 102, 103, 104, 105, 106, 107, 108, 109*
Cartier, Claude 23
Cartier, Jacques 22
Cartier, Jean-Jacques 23
Cartier, Louis 11, 20, 22
Cartier, Pierre 8, 15, 17, 20, 22
Casillot 8
Castellani 8, *11*, 28n
Castellani, Alessandro 7, 8
Castellani, Augusto 7
Castellani, Carlo Giuliano 7
Castellani, Pio Fortunato 7
Cellini, Benvenuto 7
Ceragioli Giorgio 14
Chaumet *124*
Colonna, Edouard 14
Cusi, Annibale 11, 24

Denisov-Uralski 15
Dufrène, Maurice *15*

Fabergé, Carl 11, 15
Falize, Frères 14
Falize, Lucien 12
Faraone 24
Fasano 24
Fecarotta 24
Feuillâtre, Eugène 14
Fontenay, Eugène 8
Fouquet, Alphonse *10*, 13
Fouquet, Georges 11, 12, 13, 18, 32, *38, 69, 70*
Fouquet, Jean 18, *19*
Frascarolo *127*
Froment-Maurice, François-Désiré 7

Gaillard, Lucien 14, *40*
Garrard 11, *125*
Gerard *127*
Gubelin 36, *98*

Hugo, François *24, 27*

Illario, 24

Janesich 34, *73*
Janesich, Giuseppe 14
Janesich, Leopoldo 14
Joseff of Hollywood 20

Koechert 11, *16*
Kramer, François *8*

Lacloche *71, 96*
Lalique 11
Lalique, René 12, 13, *13*, 14, *14*, 20, *39*

Marchack *121*
Marcus, Neiman 45, *120*
Marret et Baugrand 8
Martinazzi, Bruno *25, 26*, 27
Maboussin 34, 36, *66, 67, 68, 69, 112, 113, 115, 116, 117, 118, 130*
Mellerio dit Meller 8, 10, 11, 25, *47, 74, 96, 118*
Mew 26
Miranda, Vincenzo 14
Missaglia 24

Ostertag *71*
Ovcinikov 15

Petochi *122*
Phillips 8
Piel, Frères 12, 14

Ravasco, Alfredo 19
Ravasco, Giacomo 19
Rolex 36, *100*
Rubel, John *76*

Schepps, Seaman *33, 34*, 36, *126*
Schlumberger, Jean 22
Serafini *122*
Serafini, Enrico 24
Settepassi 24
Silberstein, Nina 22
Sterlé, Pierre *75, 123, 138*

Templier, Raymond 19, 32, *69*
Tiffany 8, 22, *14, 15*, 22, 32, *48, 122, 123*
Toussaint, Jeanne 15, 20, 22, *103*
Traebert & Hoeffer *112, 118*
Trifari 20

Uno a Erre 24

Van Cleef 34, 36
Van Cleef, Alfred 18
Van Cleef & Arpels 18, 19, *20, 21*, 23, *23*, 24, 25, 26, 28n, 30, *31, 32*, 34, *34*, 44, *59, 60, 61, 62, 63, 110, 111, 143*
Verdura, Fulco di 19, *19*, 21, 22, 28, *120*
Vever 10, 11, *11*, 13, 14, 28n, 30
Vever, Ernest 14
Vever, Henri 14, 18, *41*
Vever, Paul 14
Vever, Pierre 14
Viterbo, Dario 19

Webb, David 22, 28, *111, 140, 141, 142, 143, 144, 146*
Wiechmann Savioli, Flora 28
Woerffel 15

Yahr 15

This volume was printed by
Fantonigrafica - Elemond Editori Associati